HEROES & MONSTERS OF GREEK MYTH

Bernard Evslin
Dorothy Evslin
Ned Hoopes

Illustrated by William Hunter

SCHOLASTIC INC.
New York Toronto London Auckland Sydney

ISBN 0-590-41072-5

12 11 10 9 8 7 6 5 4 3 2 1   7 8 9/8 0 1/9

Printed in the U.S.A.

CONTENTS

THE PROPHECY

King Acrisius of Argos was uncertain in battle, unlucky in the hunt, and of fitful, flaring temper. He sat brooding in his throne-room.

"My daughter, Danae, grows tall and ripe," he said to himself. "Her eyes fog over when I speak to her. She is ready for a husband, but am I ready for a son-in-law? I dislike the idea and always have. A son-in-law will be a younger man waiting for me to die so he can take the throne. Perhaps he will even try to hasten that sad event.

Such things are not unknown. I loathe the idea of a son-in-law. But she is ready for a husband, and princesses must not be spinsters . . . a grave decision . . . I shall consult the oracle."

He sent to the oracle at Delphi, and the messenger returned with this prophecy: "Your daughter will bear a son who will one day kill you."

Acrisius had the messenger beheaded for bringing bad news and retired to his throne-room to continue his brooding.

"The auguries of the Pythoness are supposed to be accurate," he said to himself. "But are they? How can they be? What if I were to slay my daughter now while she is still childless; how then could she have a son to kill me? But, must I kill her to keep her childless? Is it not sufficient to forbid her male company all her days? Would I not be accomplishing the same purpose without calling upon my head the vengeance of the gods? Yes, that is a much better plan."

Thereupon he shut the beautiful young girl in a brass tower which he had specially built with no doors and only one window, a slit too narrow for a child to put an arm through. The tower was surrounded by a high spiked wall patrolled by armed sentries and savage dogs. Here Acrisius locked his daughter away, and so murderous was his temper in those days that no one dared asked him what had become of the laughing young girl.

Acrisius stayed away from the tower and waited for someone to bring him word that his daughter had died; but the news he was waiting for did not come, and he wondered what was keeping her alive. How could a girl like that, a princess used to hunting, swimming, and running free on the hillsides, a girl who had never had her wishes crossed in her life — how could she stand this imprisonment?

He rode past the brass tower which glittered in the hot sunlight. The brass helmets of the sentries glittered as did the brass collars on the necks of the huge dogs. As he rode past, he tried to see through the slit, tried to glimpse her face looking out, but the brass glitter was so bright he could not see.

The king took to watching the tower from his own castle wall, but the tower was far away, across a valley on the slope of a hill. The tower was only a splinter of light, but it seemed to glow more and more hotly until it hurt his eyes. One night he could not sleep so he went out on his castle wall in the night wind and looked out across the valley. It was a black night — no moon, no stars. The hill was only a thicker darkness. Then, suddenly, as if a torch were lighted, the tower burned clear, shining as brightly as if it were day instead of night; but the tower was lit from the inside now — the brass walls flaring more whitely, like silver, casting a dim radiance over the valley and throwing the giant shadow of trees past the hill.

Amazed and fearful, Acrisius summoned his soldiers, leaped on his horse, and rode to the tower. As they galloped toward it, the light died, and the burning tower subsided into the hillside. He led his soldiers up to the black wall. The dogs were howling. The sentries recognized the king and opened the gate. He galloped through and rode up to the slit window. Then, through the snarling of the hounds and the clatter of weapons, he heard another sound, sudden as an arrow — the sound of a baby crying.

The brass tower had no doors, having been built with no doors, so now Acrisius bade his soldiers take sledges and batter the brass walls. When the wall was breached the king stepped through and entered his daughter's cell. There in the torchlight he saw her sitting on a bench nursing a baby. She looked up at him and, smiling secretly, said, "I have named him Avenger." The word for avenger in Greek is *Perseus*.

The king's first thought was to kill mother and child, but he had a second thought. "She must be under special protection; of Apollo himself, perhaps, master of the Delphic Oracle, who does not wish his prophecies thwarted. I can die but once, true enough; but if she is being protected by the gods, and I kill her, then they will torture me through eternity. Well, we shall test the quality of her protectors."

Acrisius ordered that Danae and the baby be taken from the prison and put in a wooden boat without sails, without oars, and without food or water. "Yes," he said to himself, "we shall test the drift of events. If she is under divine patronage, the ship will be guided safely to harbor. If, on the other hand, it runs into misfortune, then, obviously, she is not being protected by the gods, and the accident of her death will bring upon me no high reprisal. Yes, I like this idea."

Thereupon, the princess and her infant son were set adrift in an empty skiff without sails and without oars. Acrisius returned to his castle and went to sleep.

Danae sat up straight in the boat and tasted the night wind as it sang past her face and whipped her hair about her shoulders. The baby laughed for joy and reached his hands to catch the glittering points of the waves. All night they drifted, and the next day, and the next night. A light rain fell, giving them water to drink; and a gull dropped a fish right into the boat, giving them food. On the second morning Danae saw that they had drifted into the lee of an island. Fishing boats stood off the shore, and fishermen were casting their nets.

She shouted. One of the slender boats sailed toward them. The fisherman was a huge, bearded fellow named Dictys who took them on board and put into shore. He was amazed by the beauty of the girl and by the impudence of the baby who pulled boldly at his beard and gurgled, but did not cry.

Dictys took mother and child to King Polydectes of the island of Seriphos. Polydectes too was amazed at the beauty of the young woman. He called her "daughter" and offered her the hospitality of the island — a house to live in and servants to wait upon her — and paid Dictys the value of a month's catch for the prize he had drawn from the sea.

THE ISLAND

Perseus grew to be a strong, fearless lad. He loved to run, to swim, to hunt, to fight with the other boys. At night, lying near the fire, he loved to hear his mother tell stories that made his brain flame with excitement — stories of the gods, of heroes, of monsters, of battles, of transformations, and of strange loves.

She told him about the three sisters called the Gorgons who were very tall and beautiful with long golden hair and golden wings. She told of how the youngest and most beautiful, named Medusa, flew into one of Athene's temples to meet with Poseidon, risen secretly from the sea. Athene, learning of this, became enraged and wove a spell upon her loom; and Poseidon, below, awakened to find that he was holding a monster in his arms. Medusa's eyes bulged as if someone were strangling her, and a swollen blackened tongue forced her mouth open, showing the yellow fangs of her teeth. Her fingers and toes were brass claws; and, worst of all, each golden hair was now a live, hissing snake. Poseidon roared with fury, cast her aside, and dived into the sea. Medusa spread her wings and flew away, weeping, to find her sisters. She was so horrible to look upon that everyone who saw her face was turned to stone. So her sisters took her to a far place, a secret place, where they lived together plotting revenge upon Athene.

Perseus made his mother tell this story over and over again for, like many children, he was fond of stories that frightened him. Best of all, though, he liked to hear of the days when his mother had been shut up in the brass tower: how she had been so sad she thought she must die; how she would look out of the slit in the wall and see nothing but a single star; how she gazed at that star, magnified by her tears, until it seemed to fill the whole sky. Its light fell keen as a sword-blade through the blackness; and, as she watched, the blade of light flashed through the slit in the brass wall filling the dark chamber with a golden light. The gold pulsed, thickened, and gathered itself into a tall column of light and formed itself into the shape of a man, but such a man as she had never seen . . . taller than any man she had ever seen with golden hair and hot golden eyes, wearing gold bracelets on his mighty arm, and carrying a volt-blue zig-zag shaft of pure light as other men carry spears.

She knelt before him. She knew he was a god, but he raised her up and said, "Yes, I am a god, but do not be afraid. I come as a man."

"He rode the golden light every night into my dungeon," she said to Perseus, "and was always gone by dawn . . . as the morning star vanishes when day begins."

"And was he my father?" asked Perseus.

"He was your father. And some day he will return to me, I know. That is why I must not take another husband, for how can I love an ordinary man, remembering him?"

"So I am the son of a god?" said Perseus.

"Yes."

"What does that make me?"

"A hero. Or a very great scoundrel." She smiled and drew the boy to her. "But let us hope that you too will rescue maidens and thwart mad kings. Sometimes, as now, with the firelight in your eyes, you look quite like him, but not so tall, not so tall."

So Perseus grew to manhood. He was the most splendid young man on all the island. He could outrace, outswim, outclimb, outfight any other lad on Seriphos; but he raged at the peacefulness of the times because he wished to try himself in battle.

Now there was one who had watched Perseus grow with great displeasure. King Polydectes, long in love with the beautiful Danae, was very eager to get rid of her fierce, young son so that he might compel her to marry him. He was a sly one, Polydectes, sly and patient and very cruel in his quiet way, and he made a skillful plan to rid himself of Perseus. He spread the news he was to marry a princess of another island and invited all the young men of Seriphos to the palace. There he asked them, as was the custom, for gifts which he would bring to the bride.

"What she loves above all else is a fine horse," he told the young men. "And I have promised her fifty splendid stallions. Will each of you select the best of his herd?"

All the young nobles promised, except Perseus, for he had nothing of his own, living as he did on the bounty of the king.

"Well, Perseus," said Polydectes. "I hear nothing but silence from you. What gift will you bring? What do you offer your king and your host who has been so generous with you and your dear mother over the years?"

Polydectes had studied Perseus well and felt sure that the boy's flaming pride would lead to some rash offer — that was the whole point of his pretended marriage and the gathering at the palace.

"I do not wish to embarrass you, Perseus," he said. "I know that you do not have the resources of these other young men; but surely I can expect a token gift, a rabbit you might snare, perhaps, or a fish you might catch."

"Oh, King," cried Perseus. "Oh, Host and Benefactor, I owe you too much gratitude to repay you with the common gift of a horse. I shall bring you the head of Medusa!"

The throne-room rang with laughter, but Polydectes' face was grave. "You choose to jest," he said. "That is not courteous for a guest of such long standing."

"I do not jest," cried Perseus. "Promises are sacred to me. I will bring you the head of Medusa, or you can take my own. This is a pact of blood, Polydectes."

Perseus turned and strode out of the throne-room. He went to a cliff overlooking the sea and, stretching his arms to the sky, said, "Oh, unknown father on Olympus — Zeus, or Apollo, or Ares, or whoever you may be who visited my mother in a shower of gold — grant your son one boon. Not the head of Medusa as I shall win that for myself, but I need to know where she is and how to get there. Please help me."

He dropped his arms and stared at the blank sky, which seemed more blue and more empty than ever before.

"Good day, brother," he heard a voice say.

He whirled around. There stood a magnificent creature with a round hat, a laughing face, a jaunty beard, winged sandals, and a golden staff entwined with serpents. Perseus knew that it was the god, Hermes, and that he should fall on his knees; but his knees would not bend, so he bowed instead.

"Our father, Zeus, is away on one of his trips," said Hermes, "but in his absence I do some of his business so I am here to serve you. What is all this now about the head of Medusa?"

Perseus told him of the rash promise he had made to Polydectes.

"Rash, indeed," murmured Hermes. "Foolhardy, in fact. It's a family trait, I suppose. God-seed and human make a strange mixture, a ferment in the blood; leads to great exploits or great folly. But . . . folly itself can be the seed of exploit. Let us see what we can do."

"I need . . ."

"Please, allow me to tell you what you need. First of all, I must tell you that sister Athene takes a special interest in your case. She is responsible for Medusa's petrifying aspect, you know, and is a sworn enemy of the Gorgon sisters. She sends you these."

Hermes reached into his pouch and pulled out a pair of Talaria, silver-winged sandals like those he himself wore. "She is not only a potent spinster," he said, "but she cobbles magically too. She made me my winged shoes, and now she has made you a pair. With these you can fly more swiftly than an eagle. Now, listen, and I will tell you what to do. Set out today. Fly north. Search until

PERSEUS

15

you find the Gray Sisters. When you find them you must force them to tell where you can find the Nymphs of the West; no one else can tell you. These Nymphs have in their keeping certain pieces of equipment which you will need to kill Medusa. Without these implements you must fail . . . Come down, Perseus! How can I speak to you when you're up there? Come down. You can practice later."

Perseus laughed with joy, turned a somersault in the air, then hovered above Hermes' head, ankle-wings whirring like the wings of a humming bird.

"I heard you," he cried. "I heard you. Gray Sisters, Nymphs of the West . . . their secrets will be my weapons. Thank you, dear brother. Thank you, Hermes. Thank Athene for me. Farewell."

He turned so that the setting sun was on his left hand and sped away, shouting, "I can fly! I can fly!"

THE QUEST

Gulls screamed, amazed, at the tall thing which flew but did not fish; falcons stooped for a closer look, then flew away; and Perseus flashed over the sea to where the land began again — a fair, rich land. He flew over fields of wheat and groves of olive trees, herds of sheep and cows, tiny villages and white cities. The land became wilder, and mountains stood up with only a few poor villages clinging to their sides. Behind the first mountains were taller crags topped with snow, the first snow Perseus had ever seen. He flew past these mountains, great forests, a plain full of rivers, and another range of mountains where neither man nor beast was to be seen. A hailstorm raged, spitting hard sharp pieces of ice at Perseus so that he had to wrap his face in his cloak as he flew.

When the storm blew itself out, Perseus found himself over the sea again, a sea of ice, not flat but full of great billows and troughs as if it had frozen all at once during a gale. The sun was a huge pale moon peering heavily over the edge of the sky. The air was so cold he could hardly breathe.

Perseus heard a thin cackling, keener than the wind. He dipped and saw three hunched figures. Thereupon, he raised his arms, pointed his toes, and plunged to earth feet-first, landing among the three Gray Sisters. Three hags they were, very long and lean. They had been born old countless years before time began and had grown older every day since. They had gray hair, never cut, so long it fell to the ground and dragged behind them as they walked. Their skin was gray; they wore no clothes, just their long gray hair; and their skin was tough and wrinkled as an alligator's. Their bare feet were like leather claws.

They sat in a close circle, scolding and jabbering and tittering. They kept snatching at each other's hands, and then Perseus saw that they had but a single eye and a single tooth for the three of them. They quarreled about them constantly, snatching them away from each other.

"Give me the eye!" cried one. "I want to see! I want to see!"

"Give me the tooth — then you will see me, see me . . . you will see me smiling."

"I want the tooth for biting. If you take the tooth, then I must have the eye."

"And what will *I* have — I, I, I? . . ."

Swiftly Perseus stepped among them, shuddering as

his hand touched their withered claws. Swiftly he seized the tooth and eye and stepped back.

"Where's the tooth? Give me the tooth!"

"Where's the eye? Give me the eye!"

"It's my turn! You've had it too long!"

"My turn . . . my turn."

"I don't have it."

"I don't have it."

"I don't have it."

"Where is it? . . . Where's the tooth? . . . Where is it, where's the eye? . . . You have it . . . You must have it . . . No, you, you, you —"

"I have it," said Perseus. "I have them both, tooth and eye."

"A stranger!"

"A thief!"

"A *man!*"

"A man! Give me the eye so that I may see him!"

"A man! Give me the tooth so that I may smile at him!"

"But *he* has them."

"Oh, yes, he has them."

"Give them back to us, young sir, so that we may see you and smile at you . . . Please . . . please . . ."

"I have your tooth and your eye," said Perseus, "and I will return them to you only in exchange for your secret."

"What secret? What secret?"

"Where do I find the Nymphs of the West?"

"Oh, that secret. No, we may not tell. No, it's a secret within a secret, and they are for keeping, not for telling. We dare not tell. It's a Gorgon secret; they will rip us to pieces if we tell."

"You belong to the Immortals and cannot die," said Perseus, "so you will crouch here through the ages with no tooth in your mouth, no eye for your head. And while you may do without smiling or without chewing, you will soon be wanting your eye. Oh, yes . . . think how long and dark the moments are for two of you when the third sister has the eye. Think of your darkness now. Think of the torment of hearing a voice and not being able to see who is speaking, and it has only been a few minutes. Think then of these minutes stretching into hours, and the hours into days, and the days into months, and the months into years — dark years, endless, boring, heavy, dark years with mind and memory growing emptier and emptier . . ."

"Give us the eye, the eye! Keep the tooth, and give us the eye!"

"There is a little jelly in my hand. It lies between my thumb and forefinger. Just a bit of pressure, a bit more, and it will be crushed, useless, unable to see. I am impatient. I must have the secret. I must know where to find the Nymphs of the West. The secret! Quickly! My finger is pressing my thumb. The jelly trembles. Can you not feel the pain in your empty sockets?"

"Aieeee . . ."

"Stop!"

"Do not crush it! We will tell . . . We will tell . . ."

"Quickly then."

And, speaking together swiftly, sobbing and tittering and sighing, they told him how to find the Nymphs of the West, who alone could give him what he needed to overcome Medusa.

Now who were these nymphs, and why were they the

guardians of this secret? . . . Ages past, when Hera married Zeus, Mother Earth gave her as a wedding present a tree that bore golden apples. Hera loved this tree very much, but after a while she found she could not keep it in her own garden for Zeus would steal the beautiful golden apples and distribute them as favors to the nymph or dryad or naiad or Titaness or human girl he happened to be courting at the time. Therefore, Hera took her magic tree and planted it at the very end of the earth, on the uttermost western isle, a place of meadows and orchards of which Zeus knew nothing. Here it was that the Titan, Atlas, stood, shoulders bowed, forehead knotted, legs braced, holding up the end of the sky. It was the three daughters of Atlas, enchantingly beautiful nymphs, whom Hera appointed to guard the treasure. It was a wise decision. These lush and fragrant dryads made better guards than any dragon or three-headed dog or sea-serpent for such monsters could be killed or chained or outwitted, but no one could get past the nymphs. They danced among the trees and shouted gay invitation to the marauder until he forgot all about his quest and came to dance with them. Then they would stroke him and give him wine to drink and dance him about in circles until he was so befuddled they could do what they chose with him. Then they would dance him to the edge of the cliff and push him into the sea. They did all this under the eye of their father, Atlas, who groaned occasionally under his burden, or stamped his foot, making the earth shake, or shrugged his shoulders, making comets fall. These strange storms of the Titan's grief gave the island a bad name; fishermen avoided it, as did sailors. Other dark secrets came to be buried here with the Nymphs of the West, and they guarded them with the same fatal skill with which they guarded the golden apples. So it was that they held the Gorgon secret.

Now, following the directions of the Gray Ones, Perseus flew west. He flew and flew over a strange misty sea until he saw the mighty hunched figure of Atlas holding up the sky. Then he dipped toward earth. The nymphs were dancing when a shadow flew over the grove.

"It's Hermes!"

"Welcome, sweet Herald! Welcome, dear cousin!"

"Come down! . . . Come quickly! Tell us all the news!"

Perseus came lower and hovered a few feet above the ground.

"*He's* not Hermes!"

"But he has Hermes' sandals. Hermes has a helper! Oh joy!"

"Not a god at all, a man! A lovely young one. All fresh and clean and lovely."

"Come down, man!"

"Come play with us, stay with us . . ."

"Come dance with us."

"You must be a great thief to steal Hermes' sandals; come tell us how you did it."

"Come down . . . Come down . . ."

Still standing on air, Perseus bowed. "Nothing would give me greater pleasure than to dance with you and tell you stories, but I have a promise to keep first, a promise to keep, weapons to get, an enemy to kill."

"Oh, you foolish men with your ridiculous quests, your oaths and enemies and impossible voyages. When will you learn to eat the fruit and spit out the pits and sleep without dreaming in the arms of your beloved? Have you ever slept in a woman's arms, sweet young sir?"

"My mother's."

"Your mother's . . . Good for a start, but not enough, not enough. Come kiss us, lad — we need kissing. It has been a dry summer."

"I cannot kiss you now," said Perseus. "Even up here I smell your apple-blossom scent, and grow bewildered, and almost forget who I am. What then if I were to come close and touch your apple-ruddy skin and drink your cider breath? I would grow drunk as bees among honeysuckle, lose my sting, and forget my oath. Please help me, Nymphs. Do not bewilder me."

"Come down . . . stop this talking, and come down . . . Forget your quest, we'll give you something better. Come down . . ."

"Look, you lovelies," said Perseus. "My father was Zeus who wooed my mother as a shaft of fire, a fountain of light. My birth was strange, and the auguries thereof. Deeds are my destiny, adventure my profession, and fighting my pleasure. Unless I fight and win, I am no good for love either. Have you ever seen a rooster after he is beaten in a fight? His comb sags, he is unfit for love, he disappoints his hens. Tell me your secret. Give me what I need to fight Medusa. Tell me where to find her, and I will go there. By the gods, I will come back with her head in my pouch. Then, then, then I will be fit for you, beautiful ones. I will come back and tell you the tale of my battle, and other tales too, and dance with you, and do your pleasure."

"He speaks well, sisters. He must be the son of a god."

"He is our cousin then. We owe him loyalty."

"The Gorgons are our cousins too."

"But so ugly. So ugly and so foul. I prefer this handsome new cousin."

"Yes, I like this one, this flyer with his bright yodel and

silver spurs. He will keep his promise, I know. He will come back and treat his chicks most nobly."

"Let us tell him . . . quickly . . . the sooner we tell, the sooner he will go, and the sooner he will return."

"I smell rain on the wind. With any luck the clouds will come and hide the eyes of Father Atlas so he cannot see us dance with the stranger and grow jealous."

"Quickly, then . . ."

They ran to Perseus and, seizing his ankles, pulled him down, and clung to him, kissing and whispering. He grew dizzy with their apple fragrance and the touch of their smooth hands and the taste of their lips; but they were not trying to befuddle him now, only to touch him because they were unable to reveal anything to anyone they could not touch. And when he put their whisperings and murmurings together he learned what he had to know about where the Gorgons dwelt and how to find Medusa.

Then they pulled him to a huge tree whose twisted roots stood half out of the ground. They searched among these roots and gave him three things: a shield of polished bronze, bright as a mirror, and he was told that he must never look at Medusa herself but only at her reflection in the shield; a sword, sickle-shaped, slender and bright as the new moon; and, lastly, a Cap of Darkness — when he put it on he disappeared altogether, and they had to grope about to catch him and to extract three kisses each for the three gifts.

He took off his Cap of Darkness and rose a bit in the air, gleaming with happiness. "Thank you, sweet Nymphs. Thank you, beautiful cousins. With these gifts I cannot fail."

"Will you keep your promise? . . . Will you come

back and tell us your story? . . . Will you come back to dance and play? Will you come back another day? . . ."

"Farewell . . . Farewell . . ." cried Perseus. He rose to the top of the trees, smiled at the sight of Hera's golden apples shining among the leaves, and resolved to steal one when he came back to take home to his mother. Then he soared away past Atlas' angry face, scowling back at him; he flashed past the mighty shoulder of the Titan and flew northward again, following the outer rim of the earth.

With the Cap of Darkness on his head, invisible as the wind, Perseus followed the curve of the dark sea that girdles the earth until he came to the Land Beyond — the Land of the Hyperboreans where the sea is a choked marsh, and the sky is low and brown, and the weeds give off a foul stench. Here, he had been told, was where the Gorgons dwelt.

He came to earth, picked his way through the rattling weeds, and came to a kind of stone orchard which looked like one of our own graveyards, a grove of statues. Looking closer, he saw that they were the old, worn-down stone figures of men and beasts; and he realized that he was looking at those who had seen Medusa's face and had been turned to stone between one breath and the next. There was a stone child running, a stone man dismounting from a stone horse, and stone lovers, touching. Perseus closed his eyes and took a deep breath. He drew his new-moon sword, held it ready, and raised his bright shield. He had to judge all his movements by the weight of things because the Cap of Darkness made him invisible even to himself.

Now, going silently as he could, he made his way among the terrible stone figures until he heard a sound of snoring. He stood still and looked. Glittering in the muddy light were brass wings. He raised his shield now, not daring to look directly, and held it as a mirror and guided himself by the reflection. In a covering of weeds lay three immensely long, bulky shapes. He saw brass wings and brass claws. Two of them slept as birds sleep with their heads tucked under their wings. But the third one slept with her face uncovered. Perseus saw the hair of her head stand up and writhe as he looked into his mirror shield, and he knew that it was Medusa. He felt the roots of his own hair prickling with horror as if they too were turning into snakes.

He kept the shield in front of his face and walked backward. The head of Medusa grew larger in the shield. He saw the snakes swelling, writhing furiously, darting their tongues, biting each other in their fury at the stranger's approach so that their blood ran like sweat over her forehead. He tilted his shield to keep her head in the center because she was directly below him now. He smelled the terrible stench of the bleeding snakes. Then he raised his sword, and, guiding himself by the reflection, struck a savage downward backhand blow, feeling the horror, anger, pride, and pleasure of battle mingling in him like a mighty potion, firing him with the furious triumph of the deed done at the very moment of the doing. His sword whipped with a magical momentum, shearing its way through the snakes, through the thick muscles and tendons, through the lizard toughness of her hide, through bone and gristle and sinew, striking off the monster head as a boy whips off the head of a dandelion in the field.

Swiftly he stooped, scooped up the head by its limp dead snakes, stuffed it into his pouch, and stood amazed for where her blood had fallen, two creatures sprang up, a warrior holding a golden sword and a beautiful white horse with golden mane and golden hooves and astounding golden wings. They were Chrysaor and Pegasus, children of Poseidon, whom Medusa had been unable to bear while she lived as a monster, and who had grown full-size in her womb.

But Perseus did not stop to look as the sisters were waking. He sprang into the air and flew off as fast as he could. The Gorgons, without losing an instant, spread their brass wings and climbed into the air and sped after him, howling. He wore the Cap of Darkness, and they could not see him; but they could smell the blood of the cut-off head and followed the spoor like hounds of the air, howling. He did not dare look back but heard the clatter of their brass wings and the snapping of their great jaws. Athene, however, had cobbled well, magically well. His sandals carried him faster than the Gorgons could fly. He drew away from them until he heard only a very faint tinkle and a cry like wind-bells chiming. Then he lost them altogether.

THE RETURN

Perseus had his prize. Medusa's head was wet and fresh in his pouch, and he was eager to get back to Seriphos to boast to his mother and make Polydectes eat his words; but first he had promises to keep.

Therefore, he flew back to the Island of the Hesperides and danced with the three Apple Nymphs. All night they danced in the orchard. They danced him as they had never danced a marauder before. They whirled him among the trees, one after the other, then all together, faster and faster. He grew drunk as a bee on their apple fragrance, their ruddy skin, and their petal touch. He was a hero! He had just finished his first quest; killed his first enemy. He was drunk on triumph too, strong with joy. He danced and strutted and gleamed. When dawn came he saluted it with a great bawling golden-voiced challenge. He celebrated like a hero, and the nymphs were so giddy with pleasure that they watched him helping himself to a golden apple from Hera's tree and only smiled.

But now the ground trembled. The sky growled thunderously. It was full morning now. The mist that had been hiding the eyes of Atlas had blown away, and the Titan looked down and saw his daughters enjoying themselves in the orchard, a sight he could not endure. He stamped his foot and made the earth shake, roared thunderously, and shrugged his shoulders making comets fall, huge flaming bolts of rock that bombarded the orchard, setting fire to the apple trees.

Perseus' blood rose as murder sang in his heart. He flew straight toward Atlas' mighty face, poised there before the gargantuan frown, and, standing on air, opened his pouch and drew out Medusa's head. The Titan turned to stone. He was a mountain now, holding up the western end of the sky. It is a mountain till this day — Mt. Atlas.

"Farewell!" shouted Perseus. "Farewell, sweet cousins . . . beautiful nymphs. Farewell, my apple-lovelies."

"Will you come again? Will you come again? . ."

"Will I not?" cried Perseus. "Every mid-summer I will return, and we will do the orchard dance again until the trees flame. Farewell . . ," and he flew away.

Southward he flew, then eastward. He crossed a desert; and now, far below, he saw the first gleam of that matchless blue that belonged to his own sea. But as he followed the Philistine shoreline which is the eastern boundary of that sea, he saw a very strange sight: a naked girl chained to a rock and, pushing toward that rock, the huge blunt head of a sea monster. The shore was black with people, an ant-swarm of people, watching.

He came lower and saw that the girl was wearing magnificent jewels. She was not weeping, but gazing straight ahead, blankly. On the shore, in front of the crowd, stood a tall man and woman wearing crowns. Perseus took a quick look and saw that the monster was still some way off. He dropped to earth and, taking off his Cap of Darkness, spoke to the man wearing the crown, "Who are you? Who is the girl, and what is the sacrifice? Is it a private ceremony or one decreed by the gods? My name is Perseus, and I wish to know."

The Queen put her face in her hands, and wept. The King said, "I am Cepheus, king of Joppa. This is my wife, Cassiepeia, and that unfortunate girl is my daughter, Princess Andromeda. My wife, foolish, boastful woman, was vain of her beauty and that of our daughter — not without reason, as you see; but she took it into her head to praise herself among the people, saying that she and Andromeda were more beautiful than any Nereiad, who, as you may know, are very jealous and enjoy the patronage of Poseidon. So they went weeping to the god of the sea, saying my wife had insulted them and demanding vengeance. Poseidon sent that sea serpent, longer than a fleet of warships, whose breath is fire, to harry our coast, destroy our shipping, burn our villages, and devour our cattle. I consulted the oracle who told me that the only way I could wipe out my wife's offense was to sacrifice my daughter to the monster. I love my daughter; but I am king, and private woe must yield to public welfare. Therefore you see her, the lovely innocent child, bound to the rock, and the beast swims near, swims near . . ."

Perseus said, "When public welfare battens on private woe, there is a great disorder in events, a filthy confusion that needs the cleanliness of a sword. Poseidon is my uncle, King, and I feel free to play with his pets."

Perseus heard the water hiss, saw spouts of steam rise as the monster's scorching breath ruffled the surface and made the sea boil. He knew they had spoken too long. Without waiting to put on his Cap of Darkness, he drew his sword and leaped into the air. Over the beast's head he flashed and fell like lightning, right onto the great scaly back. He rode the monster there, in the water, hacking at the huge head with his new-moon sword until the flames of the beast's breath were laced with blood, and the great neck split like a log under a woodman's ax.

The monster sank. Perseus flew off his back, dripping wet, flew to the rock, struck away Andromeda's chains, lifted her in his arms, and bore her gently through the air to where her mother and father stood.

"Here is your daughter," said Perseus, "but only briefly, very briefly for I claim her as my bride."

"As your bride?" shouted Cepheus. "What do you mean? Do you think I shall give my daughter, the princess, the most richly-dowered princess in the East, to an unknown vagabond?"

"I may be a vagabond," said Perseus, "but I shall not long be unknown. If you were not going to be my father-in-law, Cepheus, I should explain to you what kind of fool you are. For the sake of family harmony, however, I forbear. You were content to serve your daughter up as dead meat to this monster as the price of your wife's vanity because he came well-recommended, but you refuse to give her, warm and alive, to him who slew the monster. And why? Simply because it is unexpected. Father-in-law or not, you are a fool, Cepheus, a pitiful fool; and if by word or deed you seek to prevent me from taking your daughter, you will be a dead fool. I do not ask your leave, I am announcing my intention. Say good-by to your parents, Andromeda." Perseus lifted her in his arms again and flew away.

When he landed on Seriphos, he was amazed to find the island deserted. His mother was not at home, nor was anyone in the village. He hurried to the castle and found it blazing with light. There was a clamor of shouting and laughter and a clatter of weapons. He forced his way through a crowd of revellers, and entered the throne-room.

There he saw his mother, deathly pale, but loaded with jewels, sumptuously garbed, her beautiful bare white arm in the swarthy clutch of Polydectes. Now Perseus understood that the king had taken advantage of his absence to force Danae to marry him. He had returned just in time.

His great voice clove the uproar. "Polydectes — ho!"

All voices ceased. The king stood rigid, staring at him, his face fixed in an amazed snarl. Perseus saw him gesture to his guards. They drew their swords and stepped forward, twenty of them.

"I have brought you your gift, Polydectes," said Perseus. "Your wedding gift. Remember? Different bride, same gift."

He put his hand into his pouch. "Mother!" he shouted. "Close your eyes!"

He drew out the head of Medusa, and the throne-room became a grove of statues. Stone guards stood with stone swords up-raised. One held a javelin, about to plunge it into Perseus' back. The statue of Polydectes showed a mouth frozen in a scream. Among all the frozen shapes of terror and wrath, the white beloved figure of his mother, Danae, trembled.

He put the head in his pouch, stepped to Danae, and took her in his arms. "Be happy, mother," he said. "I am home now. Your danger is a dream, your enemy has become his own monument."

"It is the gods," she whispered. "Their whim is implacable; their caprice, our fate. Look, Perseus . . ." She led him to one of the stone figures. A bearded old man wearing a crown.

"Who is that?"

"Your grandfather, Acrisius, one of the guests, attending the nuptials of a fellow-king. He did not know that I was the bride."

"Your father? He who shut you in the tower?"

"Shut me there to thwart the prophecy . . . that his grandson would kill him."

"Delighted to oblige," said Perseus. "I never did fancy his style. Shut you up in a dungeon . . . Met another parent like that recently. Oh, that reminds me. Come home. I want you to meet your daughter . . . "

It was Perseus' own wedding night; but before he received his bride, he went to the temple of Athene and the temple of Hermes to thank them for what they had done. He made them gifts: he gave the bright shield to Athene, a very curious shield now, permanently emblazoned with the reflection of Medusa's head which had burned itself on the metal; the Cap of Darkness to Hermes. He very much wanted cap and shield for himself, but he knew that gods who give gifts expect a rich return. However, he did keep the winged sandals and the new-moon sword. He knew that his deeds had just begun and that he would have a great deal of traveling and fighting to do in days to come.

As for Medusa's head, it was too dangerous to keep. He threw it into the sea. It sank to the bottom, where it still rests, pushed here and there by the tides, passing islands, making coral where it goes.

The gods, being all-powerful, needed a more subtle praise than obedience. They preferred their intention to become man's aspiration, their caprice, his law. Athene, in particular, liked to be served this way. The gray-eyed goddess of wisdom, whose sign was the owl, taught men the arts they needed to know, not through gross decree, but through firing the brightest spirits to a white heat wherein they perceived the secret laws of nature and made discoveries and inventions.

Now, in those times, her favorite among all mortals was an Athenian named Daedalus. In the white city of the goddess Daedalus was honored among all men, and treasure after treasure flowed from his workshop — the wheel, the plough, the loom. Finally, as happens to many men, his pride raced away with his wits; and he fell into a black envy of his own nephew, Talos, a most gifted lad, whom he had taken into his workshop, and who, everyone said, was bound to follow in his footsteps.

"Aye, but he's following too fast," grumbled Daedalus to himself. "He's treading on my heels."

Daedalus, at that time, was working on a special project, a blade to cut wood more quickly than knife or ax. He had puzzled, tested, and tried many things, but nothing seemed to work. Then, one day, coming early to his workshop, he heard a curious sound. It was his nephew, Talos, who had come even earlier. He was leaning over, holding a board pinned to a low table under his knee, and swiftly cutting into it with what looked like the backbone of a fish.

The boy turned to him, smiling. "Look, uncle," he cried. "See, how splendid! Yesterday I saw a large fish stranded on the beach, half-eaten by gulls, and a notion came to me that his spine with its many sharp teeth might be just the thing we're looking for. So I took it from the fish who had no more need of it and tried it right there. I cut through a great piece of driftwood. Isn't it wonderful? Don't you think the goddess, Athene, herself, washed the fish on shore for me to see? Why are you looking at me that way, uncle? Are you not pleased?"

"Very pleased, my boy. I have long been considering your case and have been weighing how to reward you according to your merit. Well, now I think I know. But first we must go to Athene's temple to give thanks for this timely inspiration."

He took the boy by the hand and led him up the sunny road to the top of the hill, to the Acropolis where the temple of Athene stood — and still stands. Daedalus led him to the roof of the marble building; and there, as the lad stretched his arms toward heaven, Daedalus stepped softly behind him, placed his hands on his shoulders, and pushed. The boy went tumbling off the temple, off the hill, to the rocks below. But Athene who had heard the first words of the boy's prayer, caught him in mid-air, and turned him into a partridge, which flew away, drumming. She then withdrew her favor from Daedalus.

Word of the boy's death flashed through the city. Nothing could be proved against Daedalus, but he was the target of the darkest suspicions, which, curiously enough, he took as an affront, for nothing could be proved, and so he felt unjustly accused.

"Ungrateful wretches!" he cried. "I will leave this city. I will go elsewhere and find more appreciative neighbors."

He had not told them about his invention of the saw, but took the model Talos had made and set out for Crete. Arriving there, he went directly to the palace of King Minos, who, at that time, was the most powerful king in all the world, and made him a gift of the marvelous tool that could cut wood more swiftly than knife or ax. Minos, delighted, immediately appointed Daedalus Court Artificer, Smith Extraordinary, and fitted out a workshop for him with the likeliest lads for apprentices. Minos also gave the old fellow a beautiful young slave girl for his own.

Now, the Cretan women were the loveliest in the world, and Crete's court the most glittering. The capital city of Knossos made Athens seem like a little village. Women and girls alike wore topless dresses, gems in their hair, and a most beguiling scent made by slaves who had been blinded so that their noses would grow more keen. Daedalus was an honored figure at this court — and a novelty besides. The Cretans were mad for novelties so the old man was much flattered and content.

He was a special favorite with the young princesses, Ariadne and Phaedra, who loved to visit him at his workshop and watch him make things. He became very fond of the girls and made them marvelous jointed wooden dolls with springs cunningly set and coiled so that they curtsied and danced and winked their eyes. Queen Pasiphae also came to see him often. He made her a perfume flask that played music when it was uncorked and a looking glass that allowed her to see the back of her head. She spent hours with him gossiping for she was very bored.

The queen kept coaxing Daedalus to tell her why he had really left Athens for she sensed a secret; but all he would ever say was that the goddess, Athene, had withdrawn her favor, so he had been forced to leave her city.

"Goddess Athene!" she cried. "Goddess this and god that . . . What nonsense! These are old wives' tales, nursery vapors, nothing for intelligent men and women to trouble themselves about."

"Oh, my lady," cried Daedalus. "In heaven's name, take care what you say. The gods will hear, and you will be punished."

"And I took you for a sophisticated man," said the Queen. "A man of the world, a traveler, a scientist. I am disappointed in you. Gods, indeed! And are you not, my Smith, more clever by far than that lame Hephaestus? And am I not more beautiful than Aphrodite?"

She stood up tall and full-bodied, and, indeed, very beautiful. The old man trembled.

"Come here. Come closer. Look at me. Confess that I am more beautiful than the Cytherean . . . Aphrodite. Of all the gods, she is the one I disbelieve in most. Love . . . my serving maids prate of it, my daughters frisk with the idea. All through the island men meet women by rock and tree, their shadows mingle; and I, I have Minos, the crown on a stick who loves nothing but his own decrees."

"Softly, madame, softly," said Daedalus. "You are not yourself. It is midsummer, a confusing time for women; what they say then must be discounted. Your wild words will be forgiven, but please do not repeat them. Now, see what I have made for you, even as you were saying those foolish things: a parasol, lighter than a butterfly's wing, and yet so constructed that it opens by itself like a flower when it feels the sun."

But Aphrodite had heard, and she planned a terrible vengeance.

Now, Minos had always been very fond of bulls, especially white ones. He was not aware that this was a matter of heredity, that his mother, Europa, had been courted by Zeus who had assumed the guise of a white bull for the occasion. The king knew only that he liked white bulls. And, since he was in a position to indulge his preferences, he sent through all the world for the largest, the finest, and the whitest. Finally, one arrived, the most splendid bull he had ever seen. It was dazzling white, with hot black eyes, polished hooves, and coral-pink nostrils; its long sharp horns seemed to be made of jet. The king was delighted and sent for all the court to see his fine new bull.

He had no way of knowing that the animal had been

sent there by Aphrodite, and neither did Pasiphae. As soon as the queen saw the bull, she felt herself strangling with a great rush of passion. She fell violently, monstrously, in love with the bull. She came to Daedalus and told him.

"What shall I do?" she moaned. "What can I do? I'm going mad. It's tearing me to pieces. You are the cleverest man in the world. Only you can help me. Please, please, tell me what to do."

Daedalus could not resist the beautiful queen; besides she had touched his vanity. He had to prove himself clever enough to help her in her impossible wish. He thought and thought, and finally went to work. He fashioned a wooden cow with amber eyes, real ivory horns, and ivory hooves and tenderly upholstered it with the most pliant cowhide. It was hollow, and so shaped that Pasiphae could hide herself inside. He put wheels on the hooves, and springs in the wheels. That night, as the moon was rising, the great white bull saw the form of a graceful cow gliding toward him over the meadow, mooing musically.

The next morning, Pasiphae came to the workshop. She gave Daedalus a great leather bag full of gold, and said, "Be careful, old friend. This secret is a deadly one."

Both Pasiphae and Daedalus were good at keeping secrets; but this was one that had to come out for, after a while, the queen gave birth to a child, who attracted a great deal of notice as he was half bull. People derisively called him the Minotaur, or Minos' bull.

Even in his most cruel fury, Minos was a careful planner. He decided to hide his shame, knowing that the world forgets what it does not see. He had Daedalus construct a tangled maze on the palace grounds, a place of thorny hedges and sudden rooms called the Labyrinth. There were paths running this way and that, becoming corridors, plunging underground, crossing each other, crossing themselves, each one leading back to the middle, so there was no way out.

Here King Minos imprisoned Pasiphae and the Minotaur — and Daedalus too. Minos wanted to make very sure that the old craftsman would never divulge the secret of the Labyrinth so here Daedalus dwelt. His workshop was in the Labyrinth, but he did not work well. At his bench he could hear Pasiphae howling, and the hideous broken bellowing of the bull-man, who grew more loathsome and ferocious each day.

His only comfort was his son, Icarus, who, of his own free will, chose to live with him because he so loved and admired his father. It was Icarus who said to him one day, "Father, I grow weary of this maze. Let us leave this place and go to places I have not seen."

"Alas, dear boy," said Daedalus, "we cannot. It is forbidden to leave the Labyrinth."

"You know the way out, do you not? You built the thing, after all."

"Yes, certainly, I know the way out. But I dare not take it. Minos would have us put to death immediately. All I can do is petition the king to allow you to go, but I must remain."

"No. We go together."

"But I have explained to you that we cannot."

"Minos is a great king," said Icarus. "But he does not rule the whole earth. Let us leave the island. Let us leave Crete and cross the sea."

"You are mad, dear boy. How can we do this? The

sea is locked against us. Every boatman on every craft, large and small, is under strict interdict against allowing me voyage. We cannot leave the island."

"Oh, yes, we can," said Icarus. "I'll tell you how. Just make us wings."

"Wings?"

"To fly with. Like the birds — you know — wings."

"Is it possible? Can I do this?"

"Birds have them; therefore, they have been made. And anything, dear father, that has been made you can duplicate. You have made things never seen before, never known before, never dreamed before."

"I will start immediately," cried Daedalus.

He had Icarus set out baits of fish and capture a gull. Then, very carefully, he copied its wings — not only the shape of them, but the hollow bone struts, and the feathers with their wind-catching overlaps and hollow stems. And he improved a bit on the model. Finally, one day, he completed two magnificent sets of wings with real feathers plucked from the feather cloaks the Cretan dancers used. They were huge, larger than eagles' wings.

He fitted a pair to Icarus, sealing the pinions to the boy's powerful shoulders with wax. Then he donned his own.

"Good-by to Crete!" cried Icarus joyfully.

"Hear me, boy," said Daedalus. "Follow me closely and do not go off the way. Do not fly too low or the spray will wet your wings, not too high or the sun will melt them Not too high and not too low, but close by me, through the middle air."

"Oh come, come," cried Icarus, and he leaped into the air, spreading his wings and soaring off above the hedges of the Labyrinth as if he had been born with wings. Daedalus flew after him.

They flew together over the palace grounds, over the beaches, and headed out to sea. A shepherd looked up and saw them; and a fisherman looked up and saw them; and they both thought they saw gods flying. The shepherd prayed to Hermes, and the fisherman prayed to Poseidon, with glad hearts. Now, they knew, their prayers would be answered.

Icarus had never been so happy. In one leap his life had changed. Instead of groveling in the dank tunnels of the Labyrinth, he was flying, flying free under the wide bright sky in a great drench of sunlight, the first boy in the history of the world to fly. He looked up and saw a gull, and tried to hold his wings steady and float on the air as the gull was doing, as easily as a duck floats on water. He felt himself slipping, and he slipped all the way in a slanting dive to the dancing surface of the water before he could regain his balance. The water splashing his chest felt deliciously cool.

"No . . . no . . . ," he heard his father call from far above. "Not too low and not too high. Keep to the middle air . . ."

Icarus yelled back a wordless shout of joy, beat his wings, and soared up, up, toward the floating gull.

"Ha . . . ," he thought to himself. "Those things have been flying all their lives. Wait till I get a little practice. I'll outfly them all."

Crete was a brown dot behind them now; there was no land before them, just the diamond-glittering water. Old Daedalus was beating his way through the air, steadily and cautiously, trying this wing-position and that, this body angle and that, observing how the gulls thrust and soared. He kept an eye on Icarus, making mental notes about how to improve the wings once they had landed.

He felt a bit tired. The sun was heavy on his shoulders. The figures spun in his head.

"I must not go to sleep," he said to himself. "I must watch the boy. He may do something rash."

But Icarus was flying easily alongside so Daedalus hunched his shoulders, let his chin fall on his chest, and half-coasted on a column of air. He shut his eyes for a moment . . . just for a moment . . .

In that moment Icarus saw a great white swan climb past him, wings spread, shooting like a great white arrow straight for the sun and uttering a long honking call. Icarus looked after him; he had already dwindled and was a splinter of light, moving toward the sun.

"How splendid he is, flying so swiftly, so proudly, so high. How I should like to get a closer look at the sun. Once and for all I should like to see for myself what it really is. Is it a great burning eye looking through an enormous spyhole, as some Libyans say; or is it Helios driving a golden coach drawn by golden horses, as the Athenians believe; or perhaps is it a great flaming squid swimming the waters of the sky, as the barbarians say; or, maybe, as my father holds, is it a monster ball of burning gas which Apollo moves by its own motion. I think I shall go a bit closer, anyway. The old man seems to be napping. I can be up and back before he opens his eyes. How splendid if I could get a really good look at the sun and be able to tell my father something he doesn't know. How that would delight him. What a joke we will have together. Yes . . . I must follow that swan."

So Icarus, full of strength and joy, blood flaming in his veins, stretched his home-made wings and climbed after the swan. Up, up, up, he flew. The air seemed thinner, his body heavier; the sun was swollen now, filling the whole sky, blazing down at him. He couldn't see any more than he had before; he was dazed with light.

"Closer . . ." he thought. "Higher . . . closer . . . up and up . . ."

He felt the back of his shoulders growing wet.

"Yes," he thought. "This is hot work."

But the wetness was not what he supposed; it was wax — melting wax. The wax bonds of his wings were melting in the heat of the sun. He felt the wings sliding away from him. As they fell away and drifted slowly down, he gazed at them, stupefied. It was as if a great golden hand had taken him in its grasp and hurled him toward the sea. The sky tilted. His breath was torn from his chest. The diamond-hard sea was rushing toward him.

"No," he cried. "No . . . no . . ."

Daedalus, dozing and floating on his column of air, felt the cry ripping through his body like an arrow. He opened his eyes to see the white body of his son hurtling down. It fell into the sea and disappeared.

A VOICE FROM THE SEA

Young Theseus had a secret. He lived with his mother in a little hut on a wild sea-battered part of the coast called Troezen. For all his poor house and worn-out clothes, he was very proud, for he had a secret: he knew that he was the son of a king. His mother had told him the story one night when their day's catch of fish had been very bad and they were hungry.

"A king, truly," she said. "And one day you will know his name."

"But mother, then why are you not a queen and I a prince? Why don't we live in a palace instead of a hovel?"

"Politics, my son," she said sadly. "All politics . . . You're too young to understand, but your father has a cousin, a very powerful lord with fifty sons. They are waiting for your father to die so they can divide the kingdom. If they knew he had a son of his own to inherit it, they would kill the son immediately."

"When can I go to him? When can I go there and help my father?"

"When you're grown. When you know how to fight your enemies."

This was Theseus' secret . . . and he needed a secret to keep him warm in those long, cold, hard years. One of his worst troubles was his size. His being small for his age bothered him terribly for how could he become a great fighter and help his father against terrible enemies if he couldn't even hold his own against the village boys? He exercised constantly by running up and down the cliffs, swimming in the roughest seas, lifting logs and rocks, bending young trees; and indeed he grew much stronger, but he was still very dissatisfied with himself.

One day, when he had been beaten in a fight with a larger boy, he felt so gloomy that he went down to the beach and lay on the sand watching the waves, hoping that a big one would come along and cover him.

"I will not live this way!" he cried to the wind. "I will not be small and weak and poor. I will be a king, a warrior . . . or I will not be at all."

And then it seemed that the sound of the waves turned to a deep-voiced lullaby, and Theseus fell asleep — not quite asleep, perhaps, because he was watching a great white gull smashing clams open by dropping them on the rocks below. Then the bird swooped down and stood near Theseus' head looking at him, and spoke, "I can crack clams open because they are heavy. Can I do this with shrimps or scallops? No . . . they are too light. Do you know the answer to my riddle?"

"Is it a riddle?"

"A very important one. The answer is this: do not fear your enemy's size, but use it against him. Then his strength will become yours. When you have used this secret, come back, and I will tell you a better one."

Theseus sat up, rubbing his eyes. Was it a dream? Had the gull been there, speaking to him? Could it be? What did it all mean? Theseus thought and thought; then he leaped to his feet and raced down the beach, up the cliff to the village where he found the boy who had just beaten him and slapped him across the face. When the boy, who was almost as big as a man, lunged toward him swinging his big fist, Theseus caught the fist and pulled in the same direction. The boy, swung off balance by his own power, went spinning off his feet and landed headfirst.

"Get up," said Theseus. "I want to try that again."

The big fellow lumbered to his feet and rushed at Theseus, who stooped suddenly. The boy went hurtling over him and landed in the road again. This time he lay still.

"Well," said Theseus, "that was a smart gull."

One by one, Theseus challenged the largest boys of the village; and, by being swift and sure and using their own strength against them, he defeated them all.

Then, he returned to the beach and lay on the sand, watching the waves, and listening as the crashing became a lullaby. Once again, his eyes closed, then opened. The great white seagull was pacing the sand near him.

"Thank you," said Theseus.

"Don't thank me" said the gull. "Thank your father. I am but his messenger."

"My father, the king?"

"King, indeed. But not the king your mother thinks."

"What do you mean?"

"Listen now . . . Your father rules no paltry stretch of earth. His domain is as vast as all the seas, and all that is beneath them, and all that the seas claim. He is the Earthshaker, Poseidon."

"Poseidon . . . my father?"

"You are his son."

"Then why does my mother not know? How can this be?"

"You must understand, boy, that the gods sometimes fall in love with beautiful maidens of the earth, but they cannot appear to the maidens in their own forms. The gods are too large, too bright, too terrifying, so they must diguise themselves. Now, when Poseidon fell in love with your mother, she had just been secretly married to Aegeus, king of Athens. Poseidon disguised himself as her new husband, and you, you are his son. One of many, very many; but he seems to have taken a special fancy to you and plans great and terrible things for you . . . if you have the courage."

"I have the courage," said Theseus. "Let me know his will."

"Tomorrow," said the seagull, "you will receive an unexpected gift. Then you must bid farewell to your mother and go to Athens to visit Aegeus. Do not go by sea. Take the dangerous overland route, and your adventures will begin."

The waves made great crashing music. The wind

crooned. A blackness crossed the boy's mind. When he opened his eyes the gull was gone, and the sun was dipping into the sea.

"Undoubtedly a dream," he said to himself. "But the last dream worked. Perhaps this one will too."

The next morning there was a great excitement in the village. A huge stone had appeared in the middle of the road. In this stone was stuck a sword half-way up to its hilt; and a messenger had come from the oracle at Delphi saying that whoever pulled the sword from the stone was a king's son and must go to his father.

When Theseus heard this, he embraced his mother and said, "Farewell."

"Where are you going, my son?"

"To Athens. This is the time we have been waiting for. I shall take the sword from the stone and be on my way."

"But, son, it is sunk so deeply. Do you think you can? Look . . . look . . . the strongest men cannot budge it. There is the smith trying . . . And there the Captain of the Guard . . . And look . . . look at that giant herdsman trying. See how he pulls and grunts. Oh, son, I fear the time is not yet."

"Pardon me," said Theseus, moving through the crowd. "Let me through, please. I should like a turn."

When the villagers heard this, heard the short fragile-looking youth say these words, they exploded in laughter.

"Delighted to amuse you," said Theseus. "Now, watch this."

Theseus grasped the sword by the hilt and drew it from the stone as easily as though he were drawing it from a scabbard; he bowed to the crowd and stuck the sword in his belt. The villagers were too stunned to say anything.

They moved apart as he approached, making room for him to pass. He smiled, embraced his mother again, and set out on the long road to Athens.

THE ROAD

The overland road from Troezen to Athens was the most dangerous in the world. It was infested not only by bandits but also giants, ogres, and sorcerers who lay in wait for travelers and killed them for their money, or their weapons, or just for sport. Those who had to make the trip usually went by boat, preferring the risk of shipwreck and pirates to the terrible mountain brigands. If the trip overland had to be made, travelers banded together, went heavily armed, and kept watch as though on a military march.

Theseus knew all this, but he did not give it a second thought. He was too happy to be on his way . . . leaving his poky little village and his ordinary life. He was off to the great world and adventure. He welcomed the dangers that lay in wait. "The more, the better," he thought. "Where there's danger, there's glory. Why, I shall be disappointed if I am *not* attacked."

He was not to be disappointed. He had not gone far when he met a huge man in a bearskin carrying an enormous brass club. This was Corynetes, the cudgeler, terror of travelers. He reached out a hairy hand, seized Theseus by the throat and lifted his club, which glittered in the hot sunlight.

"Pardon me," said Theseus. "What are you planning to do?"

"Bash in your head."

"Why?"

"That's what I do."

"A beautiful club you have there, sir," said Theseus. "So bright and shiny. You know, it's a positive honor to have my head bashed in with a weapon like this."

"Pure brass," growled the bandit.

"Mmm . . . but is it really brass? It might be gilded wood, you know. A brass club would be too heavy to lift."

"Not too heavy for me," said the bandit, "and it's pure brass. Look . . ."

He held out his club, which Theseus accepted, smiling. Swinging it in a mighty arc he cracked the bandit's head as if it were an egg.

"Nice balance to this," said Theseus. "I think I'll keep it." He shouldered the club and walked off.

The road ran along the edge of the cliff above the burning blue sea. He turned a bend in the road and saw a man sitting on a rock. The man held a great battle-ax in his hand; he was so large that the ax seemed more like a hatchet.

"Stop!" said the man.

"Good day," said Theseus.

"Now listen, stranger, everyone who passes this way washes my feet. That's the toll. Any questions?"

"One. Suppose I don't?"

"Then I'll simply cut off your head," said the man, "unless you think that little twig you're carrying will stop this ax."

"I was just asking," said Theseus. "I'll be glad to wash your feet, sir. Personal hygiene is very important, especially on the road."

"What?"

"I said I'll do it."

Theseus knelt at the man's feet and undid his sandals, thinking hard. He knew who this man was; he had heard tales of him. This was Sciron who was notorious for keeping a pet turtle that was as large for a turtle as Sciron was for a man and was trained to eat human flesh. This giant turtle swam about at the foot of the cliff waiting for Sciron to kick his victims over. Theseus glanced swiftly down the cliffside. Sure enough, he saw the great blunt head of the turtle lifted out of the water, waiting.

Theseus took Sciron's huge foot in his hand, holding it by the ankle. As he did so, the giant launched a mighty kick. Theseus was ready. When the giant kicked, Theseus pulled, dodging swiftly out of the way as the enormous body hurtled over him, over and down, splashing the water cliff-high as it hit. Theseus saw the turtle swim toward the splash. He arose, dusted off his knees, and proceeded on his journey.

The road dipped now, running past a grove of pines. "Stop!"

He stopped. There was another huge brute of a man facing him. First Theseus thought that Sciron had climbed back up the cliff somehow; but then he realized that this must be Sciron's brother, of whom he had also heard. This fellow was called Pityocamptes, which means "pine-bender." He was big enough and strong enough to press pine trees to the ground. It was his habit to bend a tree just as a passerby approached and ask the newcomer to hold it for a moment. The traveler, afraid not to oblige, would grasp the top of the tree. Then Pityocamptes with a great jeering laugh would release his hold. The pine tree would spring mightily to its full height, flinging the victim high in the air, so high that the life was dashed out of him when he hit the ground. Then the bandit would search his pockets, chuckling all the while, as he was a great joker. Now he said to Theseus, "Wait, friend. I want you to do me a favor."

He reached for a pine tree and bent it slowly to earth like an enormous bow. "Just hold this for a moment like a good fellow, will you?"

"Certainly," said Theseus.

Theseus grasped the tree, set his feet, clenched his teeth, let his mind go dark and all his strength flow downward, through his legs, into the earth, anchoring him to the earth like a rock. Pityocamptes let go, expecting to see Theseus fly into the air. Nothing happened. The pine stayed bent. The lad was holding it, legs rigid, arms trembling. The giant could not believe his eyes. He thought he must have broken the pine while bending it. He leaned his head closer to see. Then Theseus let go. The tree snapped up, catching the giant under the chin, knocking him unconscious. Theseus bent the tree again, swiftly bound the giant's wrists to it. He pulled down another pine and tied Pityocamptes' legs to that . . . and then let both pines go. They sprang apart. Half of Pityocamptes hung from one tree, half from the other. Vultures screamed with joy and fed on both parts impartially. Theseus wiped the pine tar from his hands and continued on his way.

By now it was nightfall, and he was very weary. He came to an inn where light was coming from the window, smoke from the chimney. But it was not a cozy sight as the front yard was littered with skulls and other bones.

"They don't do much to attract guests," thought Theseus. "Well . . . I'm tired. It has been a gruesome day. I'd just as soon go to bed now without any more fighting. On the other hand, if an adventure comes my way, I must not avoid it. Let's see what this bone-collector looks like."

He strode to the door and pounded on it, crying, "Landlord! Landlord, ho!"

The door flew open. In it was framed a greasy-looking giant, resembling Sciron and the pine-bender, but older, filthier, with long, tangled gray hair and a blood-stained gray beard. He had great meaty hands like grappling hooks.

"Do you have a bed for the night?" said Theseus.

"A bed? That I have. Come with me."

He led Theseus to a room where a bed stood — an enormous ugly piece of furniture, hung with leather straps, and chains, and shackles.

"What are all those bolts and bindings for?" said Theseus.

"To keep you in bed until you've had your proper rest."

"Why should I wish to leave the bed?"

"Everyone else seems to. You see, this is a special bed, exactly six feet long from head to foot. And I am a very neat, orderly person. I like things to fit. Now, if the guest is too short for the bed, we attach those chains to his ankles and stretch him. Simple."

"And if he's too long?" said Theseus.

"Oh, well then we just lop off his legs to the proper length."

"I see."

"But don't worry about that part of it. You look like a stretch job to me. Go ahead, lie down."

"And if I do, then you will attach chains to my ankles and stretch me — if I understand you correctly."

"You understand me fine. Lie down."

"But all this stretching sounds uncomfortable."

"You came here. Nobody invited you. Now you've got to take the bad with the good."

"Yes, of course," said Theseus. "I suppose if I decided not to take advantage of your hospitality . . . I suppose you'd *make* me lie down, wouldn't you?"

"How? Show me."

The inn-keeper, whose name was Procrustes, reached out a great hand, put it on Theseus' chest, and pushed him toward the bed. Theseus took his wrist, and, as the big man pushed, he pulled . . . in the swift shoulder-turning downward snap he had taught himself. Procrustes flew over his shoulder and landed on the bed. Theseus bolted him fast, took up an ax, and chopped off his legs as they dangled over the footboards. And then, because he did not wish to see the fellow suffer, chopped off his head too.

"As you have done by travelers, so are you done by," said Theseus. "You have made your bed, old man. Now lie on it."

He put down the ax, picked up his club, and resumed his journey, deciding to sleep in the open because he found the inn unpleasant.

ATHENS

Athens was not yet a great city in those days, but it was far more splendid than any Theseus had seen. He found it quite beautiful with arbors and terraces and marble temples. After the adventures of the road, however, he found it strangely dull. He suffered too from humiliation for, although he was the king's son, his father was in a very weak position so he could not be a real prince. It was his father's powerful cousin, the tall black-browed Pallas with his fifty fierce sons, who actually ran things. Their estate was much larger and finer than the castle, their private army stronger than the Royal Guard, and Theseus could not bear it.

"Why was I given the sign?" he stormed. "Why did I pull the sword from the stone and come here to Athens? To skulk in the castle like a runaway slave? What difference does it make, father, how *many* there are? After we fight them, there will be many less. Let's fight! right now!"

"No," said Aegeus, "we cannot. Not yet. It would not be a battle, it would be suicide. They must not know you are here. I am sorry now I had you come all the way to Athens. It is too dangerous. I should have kept you in some little village somewhere, outside of town, where we could have seen each other every day, but where you would not be in such danger."

"Well, if I am no use here, let me go to Crete!" cried Theseus. "If I can't fight our enemies at home, let me try my hand abroad."

"Crete! . . . Oh, my dear boy, no, no . . ," and the old man fell to lamenting for it was in these days that Athens, defeated in a war with Crete, was forced by King Minos to pay a terrible tribute. He demanded that each year the Athenians send him seven of their most beautiful maidens, seven of their strongest young men. These were taken to the Labyrinth and offered to the monster who lived there — the dread Minotaur, half man and half bull — son of Pasiphae and the bull she had fallen in love with. Year after year they were taken from their parents, these seven maidens and seven youths, and were never heard of again. Now the day of tribute was approaching again.

Theseus offered to go himself as one of the seven young men and take his chances with the monster. He kept hammering at his father, kept producing so many arguments, was so electric with impatience and rage, that finally his father consented, and the name Theseus was entered among those who were to be selected for tribute. The night before he left, he embraced Aegeus and said, "Be of good heart, dear sire. I traveled a road that was supposed to be fatal before and came out alive. I met quite a few unpleasant characters on my journey and had a few anxious moments, but I learned from them that the best weapon you can give an enemy is your own fear. So . . . who can tell. I may emerge victorious from the Labyrinth and lead my companions home safely. Then I will be known to the people of Athens and will be able to rouse them against your tyrant cousins and make you a real king."

"May the gods protect you, son," said Aegeus. "I shall sacrifice to Zeus and to Ares, and to our own Athene, every day, and pray for your safety."

"Don't forget Poseidon," said Theseus.

"Oh, yes, Poseidon too," said Aegeus. "Now do this for me, son. Each day I shall climb the Hill of the Temple, and from there watch over the sea . . . watching for your ship to return. It will depart wearing black sails, as all the sad ships of tribute do; but if you should overcome the Minotaur, please, I pray you, raise a white sail. This will tell me that you are alive and save a day's vigil."

"That I will do," said Theseus. "Watch for the white sail . . ."

CRETE

All Athens was at the pier to see the black-sailed ship depart. The parents of the victims were weeping and tearing their clothing. The maidens and the young men, chosen for their beauty and courage, stood on the deck trying to look proud; but the sound of lamentation reached them, and they wept to see their parents weep. Then Theseus felt the cords of his throat tighten with rage. He stamped his foot on the deck and shouted, "Up anchor, and away!" as though he were the captain of the vessel. The startled crew obeyed, and the ship moved out of the harbor.

Theseus immediately called the others to him. "Listen to me," he said. "You are not to look upon yourselves as victims, or victims you will surely be. The time of tribute has ended. You are to regard this voyage not as a submission but as a military expedition. Everything will change, but first you must change your own way of looking at things. Place your faith in my hands, place yourselves under my command. Will you?"

"We will!" they shouted.

"Good. Now I want every man to instruct every girl in the use of the sword and the battle-ax. We may have to cut our way to freedom. I shall also train you to respond to my signals — whistles, hand-movements — for if we work as a team, we may be able to defeat the Minotaur and confound our enemies."

They agreed eagerly. They were too young to live without hope, and Theseus' words filled them with courage. Every day he drilled them, man and maiden alike, as though they were a company of soldiers. He taught them to wrestle in the way he had invented. And this wild young activity, this sparring and fencing, so excited the crew, that they were eager to place themselves under the young man's command.

"Yes," he said. "I will take your pledges. You are Athenians. Right now that means you are poor, defeated, living in fear. But one day 'Athenian' will be the proudest name in the world, a word to make warriors quake in their armor, kings shiver upon their thrones!"

Now Minos of Crete was the most powerful king in all the world. His capital, Knossos, was the gayest, richest, proudest city in the world; and the day, each year, when the victims of the Minotaur arrived from Athens, was always a huge feast-day. People mobbed the streets — warriors with shaven heads and gorgeous feathered cloaks, women in jewels and topless dresses, children, farmers, great swaggering bullherders, lithe bullfighters, dwarfs, peacocks, elephants, and slaves, slaves, slaves from every country known to man. The streets were so jammed no one could walk freely, but the King's Guard kept a lane open from quayside to Palace. And here, each year, the fourteen victims were marched so that the whole city could see them marched past the crowds to the Palace to be presented to the king, who approved their beauty before giving them to the Minotaur.

On this day of arrival, the excited harbormaster came puffing to the castle, fell on his knees before the throne, and gasped, "Pity, great king, pity . . ."

And then in a voice strangled with fright the harbormaster told the king that one of the intended victims, a young man named Theseus, demanded a private audience with Minos before he would allow the Athenians to disembark.

"My warships!" thundered Minos. "The harbor is full of triremes. Let the ship be seized, and this Theseus and his friends dragged here through the streets."

"It cannot be, your majesty. Their vessel stands over the narrow neck of the harbor. And he swears to scuttle it right there, blocking the harbor, if any of our ships approach."

"Awkward . . . very awkward," murmured Minos. "Quite resourceful for an Athenian, this young man. Worth taking a look at. Let him be brought to me."

Thereupon Theseus was informed that the king agreed to see him privately. He was led to the Palace, looking about eagerly as he was ushered down the lane past the enormous crowd. He had never seen a city like this. It made Athens look like a little fishing village. He was excited and he walked proudly, head high, eyes flashing. When he came to the Palace, he was introduced to the king's daughters, two lovely young princesses, Ariadne and Phaedra.

"I regret that my queen is not here to greet you," said Minos. "But she has become attached to her summer house in the Labyrinth and spends most of her time there."

The princesses were silent, but they never took their eyes off Theseus. He could not decide which one he preferred. Ariadne, he supposed — the other was really still a little girl. But she had a curious cat-faced look about her that intrigued him. However, he could not give much thought to this; his business was with the king.

Finally, Minos signaled the girls to leave the room, and motioned Theseus toward his throne. "You wanted to see me alone," he said. "Here I am. Speak."

"I have a request, your majesty. As the son of my

father, Aegeus, King of Athens, and his representative in this court, I ask you formally to stop demanding your yearly tribute."

"Oh, heavens," said Minos. "I thought you would have something original to say. And you come with this threadbare old petition. I have heard it a thousand times and refused it a thousand times."

"I know nothing of what has been done before," said Theseus. "But only of what I must do. You laid this tribute upon Athens to punish the city, to show the world that you were the master. But it serves only to degrade you and show the world that you are a fool."

"Feeding you to the Minotaur is much too pleasant a finale for such an insolent rascal," said Minos. "I shall think of a much more interesting way for you to die — perhaps several ways."

"Let me explain what I mean," said Theseus. "Strange as it seems, I do not hate you. I admire you. You're the most powerful king in the world and I admire power. In fact, I intend to imitate your career. So what I say, I say in all friendliness, and it is this: when you take our young men and women and shut them in the Labyrinth to be devoured by the Minotaur, you are making the whole world forget Minos, the great general Minos, the wise king. What you are forcing upon their attention is Minos, the betrayed husband, the man whose wife disliked him so much she eloped with a bull. And this image of you is what people remember. Drop the tribute, I say, and you will once again live in man's mind as warrior, law-giver, and king."

"You are an agile debater," said Minos, "as well as a very reckless young man, saying these things to me. But there is a flaw in your argument. If I were to drop the tribute, my subjects would construe this as an act of weakness. They would be encouraged to launch conspiracies against me. Other countries under my sway would be encouraged to rebel. It cannot be done."

"I can show you a graceful way to let the tribute lapse. One that will not be seen as a sign of weakness. Just tell me how to kill the monster."

"Kill the monster, eh? And return to Athens a hero? And wipe out your enemies there? And then subdue the other cities of Greece until you become leader of a great alliance? And then come visit me again with a huge fleet and an enormous army, and topple old Minos from his throne . . ? Do I describe your ambitions correctly?"

"The future does not concern me," said Theseus. "I take one thing at a time. And the thing that interests me now is killing the Minotaur."

"Oh, forget the Minotaur," said Minos. "How do you know there is one? How do you know it's not some maniac there who ties sticks to his head? Whatever it is, let him rot there in the Labyrinth with his mad mother. I have a better plan for you. My sons are dead. My daughter Ariadne, I notice, looks upon you with favor. Marry her, and become my heir. One day you will rule Crete and Athens both . . . and all the cities of the sea."

"Thank you, sir. I appreciate your offer. But I came here to fight a monster."

"You are mad."

"Perhaps. But this is the only way I know how to be. When I am your age, when the years have thinned my blood, when rage has cooled into judgment, then I will go in for treaties, compromises. Now, I must fight."

"Why is the young fool so confident?" thought Minos to himself. "He acts like a man who knows he is protected by the gods. Can it be true what they say? Is he really the son of Poseidon? Do I have that kind of enemy on my hands? If so, I will make doubly sure to get rid of him."

Then he said aloud, "You are wrong to refuse my offer. I suppose you are made so wildly rash by some old wives' gossip in your little village that you are the son of this god or that. Those mountain villages of yours, they're ridiculous. Every time a child does something out of the way, all the crones and hags get together and whisper, 'He's the son of a god, really the son of a god.' Is that the way of it? Tell the truth now."

"My truth," said Theseus, "is that I am the son of Poseidon."

"Poseidon, eh? No less. Well, how would you like to prove it?"

"Why should I care to prove it? *I* know. That's enough for me. The whole world has heard that you are the son of Zeus, who courted your mother, Europa, in the guise of a white bull. Everyone has heard this tale; few disbelieve it. But can you prove it?"

"Come with me," said Minos.

He led him out of the Palace, beyond the wall, to a cliff overlooking the sea. He stood tall, raised his arms, and said, "Father Zeus, make me a sign."

Lightning flashed so furiously that the night became brighter than day, and the sky spoke in thunder. Then Minos dropped his arms; the light stopped pulsing in the sky, and the thunder was still.

"Well," said Minos. "Have I proved my parentage?"

"It's an impressive display. I suppose it proves something."

"Then show me you are the son of Poseidon."

Minos took the crown from his head and threw it over

the cliff into the sea. They heard the tiny splash far below.

"If you are his son, the sea holds no terror for you. Get me my crown," said Minos.

Without a moment's hesitation, Theseus stepped to the edge of the cliff and leaped off. As he fell, he murmured, "Father, help me now."

Down he plunged, struck the black water and went under, shearing his way through until he felt his lungs bursting. But he did not kick toward the surface. He let out the air in his chest in a long tortured gasp, and then, breathed in. No strangling rush of water, but a great lungfull of sweet cool air . . . and he felt himself breathing as naturally as a fish. He swam down, down, and as he swam his eyes became accustomed to the color of the night sea; he moved in a deep green light. And the first thing he saw was the crown gleaming on the bottom. He swam down and picked it up.

Theseus stood on the ocean bottom holding the crown in his hand and said, "All thanks, Father Poseidon."

He waited there for the god to answer him, but all he saw were dark gliding shapes, creatures of the sea passing like shadows. He swam slowly to the surface, climbed the cliff, and walked to where Minos was waiting.

"Your crown, sir."

"Thank you."

"Are you convinced now that Poseidon is my father?"

"I am convinced that the water is more shallow here than I thought. Convinced that you are lucky."

"Luck? Is that not another word for divine favor?"

"Perhaps. At any rate, I am also convinced that you are a dangerous young man. So dangerous that I am forced to strip you of certain advantages allowed those who face the Minotaur. You will carry neither sword nor ax, but only your bare hands . . . And your luck, of course. I think we will not meet again. So farewell." He whistled sharply. His Royal Guard appeared, surrounded Theseus, and marched him off to a stone tower at the edge of the Labyrinth. There they locked him up for the night.

An hour before dawn Ariadne appeared in his cell and said, "I love you, Theseus. I will save you from death if you promise to take me back to Athens with you."

"And how do you propose to save me, lovely princess?"

"Do you know what the Labyrinth is? It is a hedge of a thousand lanes, all leading in, and only one leading out. And this one is so concealed, has so many twists and turns and secret windings that no one can possibly find his way out. Only I can travel the Labyrinth freely. I will lead you in and hide you. I will also lead you around the central chamber where the Minotaur is and lead you out again. You will not even see the monster. Since no one has ever found his way out of the maze, Minos will assume that you have killed the Minotaur, and you will have a chance to get to your ship and escape before the trick is discovered. But you must take me with you."

"It cannot be," said Theseus.

"Don't you believe me? It's all true. Look . . ."

She took from her tunic a ball of yellow silk thread and dropped it on the floor. The ball swiftly rolled across the room, unwinding itself as it went. It rolled around the bench, wrapped itself around one of Theseus' ankles, rolled up the wall, across the ceiling and down again. Then Ariadne tugged sharply on her end of the thread, and the ball reversed itself, rolling back the way it had come, reeling in its thread as it rolled. Back to Ariadne it rolled and leaped into her hand.

"This was made for me by old Daedalus," said Ariadne. "It was he who built the Labyrinth, you know. And my father shut him up in it too. I used to go visit him there. He made me this magic ball of thread so that I would always be able to find my way to him, and find my way back. He was very fond of me."

"I'm getting very fond of you too," said Theseus.

"Do you agree?" cried Ariadne. "Will you let me guide you in the Labyrinth and teach you how to avoid the monster, and fool my father. Say you will. Please . . ."

"I'll let you guide me through the maze," said Theseus. "Right to where the monster dwells. You can stay there and watch the fight. And when it's over, you can lead me back."

"No, no, I won't be able to. You'll be dead! It's impossible for you to fight the Minotaur."

"It is impossible for me not to."

"You won't even be armed."

"I have always traveled light, sweet princess, and taken my weapons from the enemy. I see no reason to change my habits now. Are you the kind of girl who seeks to change a man's habits? If you are, I don't think I will take you back to Athens."

"Oh, please, do not deny me your love," she said. "I will do as you say."

The next morning when the Royal Guard led Theseus out of the tower and forced him into the outer lane of the Labyrinth, Ariadne was around the first bend, waiting. She tied one end of the thread to a branch of the hedge, then dropped the ball to the ground. It rolled slowly, unwinding; they followed, hand in hand. It was pleasant, walking in the Labyrinth. The hedge grew tall above their heads and was heavy with little white sweet-smelling flowers. The lane turned and twisted and turned again, but the ball of thread ran ahead, and they followed it. Theseus heard a howling.

"Sounds like the wind," he said.

"No, it is not the wind. It is my mad mother, howling."

They walked farther. They heard a rumbling, crashing sound.

"What's that?"

"That is my brother. He's hungry."

They continued to follow the ball of thread. Now the hedges grew so tall the branches met above their heads, and it was dark. Ariadne looked up at him, sadly. He bent his head and brushed her lips in a kiss.

"Please don't go to him," she said. "Let me lead you out now. He will kill you. He has the strength of a bull and the cunning of a man."

"Who knows?" said Theseus. "Perhaps he has the weakness of a man and the stupidity of a bull." He put his hand over her mouth. "Anyway, let me think so because I must fight him, you see, and I'd rather not frighten myself beforehand."

The horrid roaring grew louder and louder. The ball of thread ran ahead, ran out of the lane, into an open space. And here, in a kind of meadow surrounded by the tall hedges of the Labyrinth, stood the Minotaur.

Theseus could not believe his eyes. The thing was more fearsome than in his worst dreams. What he had expected was a bull's head on a man's body. What he saw was something about ten feet tall shaped like a man, like an incredibly huge and brutally muscular man, but covered with a short dense brown fur. It had a man's face, but a squashed, bestialized one, with poisonous red eyes, great blunt teeth, and thin leathery lips. Sprouting out of its head were two long heavy polished horns. Its feet were hooves, razor sharp; its hands were shaped like a man's hands, but much larger and hard as horn. When it clenched them they were great fists of bone.

It stood pawing the grass with a hoof, peering at Theseus with its little red eyes. There was a bloody slaver on its lips.

Now, for the first time in all his battles, Theseus became unsure of himself. He was confused by the appearance of the monster. It filled him with a kind of horror that was beyond fear, as if he were wrestling a giant spider. So when the monster lowered its head and charged, thrusting those great bone lances at him, Theseus could not move out of the way.

There was only one thing to do. Drawing himself up on tiptoe, making himself as narrow as possible, he leaped into the air and seized the monster's horns. Swinging himself between the horns, he somersaulted onto the Minotaur's head, where he crouched, gripping the horns with desperate strength. The monster bellowed with rage and shook its head violently. But Theseus held on. He thought his teeth would shake out of his head; he felt his eyeballs rattling in their sockets. But he held on.

Now, if it can be done without one's being gored, somersaulting between the horns is an excellent tactic when fighting a real bull; but the Minotaur was not a real bull; it had hands. So when Theseus refused to be shaken off but stood on the head between the horns trying to dig his heels into the beast's eyes, the Minotaur stopped shaking his head, closed his great horny fist, big as a cabbage and hard as a rock, and struck a vicious backward blow, smashing his fist down on his head, trying to squash Theseus as you squash a beetle.

This is what Theseus was waiting for. As soon as the

fist swung toward him, he jumped off the Minotaur's head, and the fist smashed between the horns, full on the skull. The Minotaur's knees bent, he staggered and fell over; he had stunned himself. Theseus knew he had only a few seconds before the beast would recover his strength. He rushed to the monster, took a horn in both hands, put his foot against the ugly face, and putting all his strength in a sudden tug, broke the horn off at the base. He leaped away. Now he, too, was armed, and with a weapon taken from the enemy.

The pain of the breaking horn goaded the Minotaur out of his momentary swoon. He scrambled to his feet, uttered a great choked bellow, and charged toward Theseus, trying to hook him with his single horn. Bone cracked against bone as Theseus parried with his horn. It was like a duel now, the beast thrusting with his horn, Theseus parrying, thrusting in return. Since the Minotaur was much stronger, it forced Theseus back — back until it had Theseus pinned against the hedge. As soon as he felt the first touch of the hedge, Theseus disengaged, ducked past the Minotaur, and raced to the center of the meadow, where he stood, poised, arm drawn back. For the long pointed horn made as good a javelin as it did a sword, and so could be used at a safer distance.

The Minotaur whirled and charged again. Theseus waited until he was ten paces away, and then whipped his arm forward, hurling the javelin with all his strength. It entered the bull's neck and came out the other side. But so powerful was the Minotaur's rush, so stubborn his bestial strength, that he trampled on with the sharp horn through his neck and ran right over Theseus, knocking him violently to the ground. Then it whirled to try to stab Theseus with its horn; but the blood was spouting fast now, and the monster staggered and fell on the ground beside Theseus.

Ariadne ran to the fallen youth. She turned him over, raised him in her arms; he was breathing. She kissed him. He opened his eyes, looked around, and saw the dead Minotaur; then he looked back at her and smiled. He climbed to his feet, leaning heavily on Ariadne.

"Tell your thread to wind itself up again, Princess. We're off for Athens."

When Theseus came out of the Labyrinth there was an enormous crowd of Cretans gathered. They had heard the sound of fighting, and, as the custom was, had gathered to learn of the death of the hostages. When they saw the young man covered with dirt and blood, carrying a broken horn, with Ariadne clinging to his arm, they raised a great shout.

Minos was there, standing with his arms folded. Phaedra was at his side. Theseus bowed to him and said, "Your majesty, I have the honor to report that I have rid your kingdom of a foul monster."

"Prince Theseus," said Minos. "According to the terms of the agreement, I must release you and your fellow hostages."

"Your daughter helped me, king. I have promised to take her with me. Have you any objection?"

"I fancy it is too late for objections. The women of our family haven't had much luck in these matters. Try not to be too beastly to her."

"Father," said Phaedra, "she will be lonesome there in far-off Athens. May I not go with her and keep her company?"

"You too?" said Minos. He turned to Theseus. "Truly,

young man, whether or not Poseidon has been working for you, Aphrodite surely has."

"I will take good care of your daughters, king," said Theseus. "Farewell."

And so, attended by the Royal Guard, Theseus, his thirteen happy companions, and the two Cretan princesses, walked through the mobbed streets from the Palace to the harbor. There they boarded their ship.

It was a joyous ship that sailed northward from Crete to Athens. There was feasting and dancing night and day. And every young man aboard felt himself a hero too, and every maiden a princess. And Theseus was lord of them all, drunk with strength and joy. He was so happy he forgot his promise to his father — forgot to tell the crew to take down the black sail and raise a white one.

King Aegeus, keeping a lonely watch on the Hill of the Temple, saw first a tiny speck on the horizon. He watched it for a long time and saw it grow big and then bigger. He could not tell whether the sail was white or black; but as it came nearer, his heart grew heavy. The sail seemed to be dark. The ship came nearer, and he saw that it wore a black sail. He thought that his son was dead.

"I have killed him," he cried. "In my weakness, I sent him off to be killed. I am unfit to be king, unfit to live. I must go to Tartarus immediately and beg his pardon there."

And then the old king leaped from the hill, dived through the steep air into the sea far below, and was drowned — giving that lovely blue, fatal stretch of water its name for all time, the Aegean Sea.

Theseus, upon his return to Athens, was hailed as king. The people worshipped him. He swiftly raised an army, wiped out his powerful cousins, and then led the Athenians forth into many battles, binding all the cities of Greece together in an alliance. One day sometime later he returned to Crete to reclaim the crown of Minos which once he had recovered from the sea.

ON THE MOUNTAIN

Atalanta's bad luck began when she was born, for her father, the king of Arcadia, wanted a son. In his rage at being given a girl, he ordered that she be left on a mountainside to die. The nearest mountain, as it happened, was in the neighboring country of Calydon so the infant girl was taken here. She was stuck in a cleft of rock and left under the cold stars.

Her cries attracted the attention of a she-bear who was prowling the slope looking for a lost cub. The huge blunt-headed furry beast came nosing up to the squalling infant. It was not her cub, but it was alive; its tiny hand came out and clutched the shaggy ruff of the bear. She lifted the baby gently in her jaws and carried it off to her cave.

Across the valley from the she-bear's cave stood a castle belonging to the king of Calydon, whose son named Meleager also had a curious infancy. When he was three days old, his mother, Queen Althaea, was visited by a tall, gray-faced old woman carrying a pair of long silver shears in her hand. The queen knew it was Atropos, one of the three Fates, and she was afraid. The old woman said to her, "We are being kind to you. We usually strike without warning. See that stick of wood at the edge of the fire, just beginning to burn? Your son's life will last just as long as that stick remains unburned."

Atropos then disappeared.

Althaea leaped to the fireplace, snatched the stick out of the flames, and locked it in a great brass chest.

The prince was not the same as other children; from the time he could run he was interested in nothing but hunting. His father was delighted with the boy. He had his smith make a tiny spear and a bow that shot arrows no larger than darts, but they were not toys. Meleager practiced with them constantly and learned to use them well. As soon as he could sit on a pony, he followed his father on the hunt; and by the time he was a young man, he was accounted the best hunter in all Greece. He had taken enough lion, wolf, and bear pelts to cover the floors of the huge castle. The walls were hung with stag-horns and bear-tusks. In the lowlands he hunted on horseback; among the hills, on foot.

However, Meleager was a worry to his parents in one respect because he snubbed all the eligible maidens of Calydon.

"Father, please," he said. "I can't stand them . . . soft, squealing little things; no good with spear or bow, hopeless on horseback. I'll not marry until I find a girl who can hunt by my side."

One day, on the slope of a near mountain, he cornered an enormous bear. It lashed out with its great paw and struck Meleager's javelin from his hand. Then the bear charged so swiftly that the lad barely had time to draw his dagger before the beast was upon him. He slipped under the swinging paws and stabbed the bear in the back of its neck, and then was knocked off his feet by its backward lurch. As he sprang up, he was just in time to see the bear charging away up the slope, the dagger still stuck in his neck, blood welling from the wound. Meleager scrambled after it.

Despite his terrible wound, the beast moved swiftly, and Meleager soon lost sight of him; but he followed the trail of blood, knowing that it was only a question of time till the animal dropped. It had been early morning when he fought the bear; now the burning summer sun was directly overhead, and he was panting with heat as he followed the trail of blood. Then, rounding a spur of rock, he saw an amazing sight: a tall, bare-legged maiden came running down the hill with long strides, wearing a great shaggy fur cloak. Just as he thought, "Why is she wearing that heavy cloak in all this heat?" he saw that blood was dripping from her and realized that it was not a fur cloak she was wearing, but that on her back was the huge bear he had fought. The animal's head was lolling on her shoulder, its blood was dripping on her; he saw the hilt of his dagger still protruding from its neck.

He stood in the path. The girl stopped. Gently she slid the body of the bear to the ground, straightened, and faced him. He was dazed by her beauty. She was as tall as he, long-legged as a deer, clad in a brief tunic of wolf-skin, her rich brown hair hanging to her knees. Her face was streaked with dirt, her bare arms and shoulders blotched with blood; he knew instantly that this was the one girl in the world for him.

"That's my bear," he said. "But I give him to you."

"Your bear?"

"My kill. That's my dagger sticking from his neck. I've been tracking him all day. But you can . . ."

He was interrupted by her hoarse cry of rage. She stooped swiftly, picked up a huge stone as if it were a pebble, and hurled it at his head. He ducked but felt it graze his hair. He saw her bend again and pull his dagger from the bear's neck. Then, holding the dagger, she came slowly toward him.

"This bear is my brother," she said. "You have killed my brother. Now I must kill you."

"Sweet maiden . . ."

"Sweet? You'll find me bitter as death. Come, pick up your spear and fight."

He picked up his spear and hurled it in the same motion. It sang through the air and split a sapling neatly in two. Then he turned and stood facing her with empty hands.

"Why have you disarmed yourself?" she said. "I mean to kill you."

"Come ahead then. Use the dagger, by all means. It will make things more even."

She howled with rage, and flung the dagger away. "I need no favors from you!" she cried. "I'll do it with my bare hands."

She rushed upon him. He caught her by the arms and tried to handle her gently; but it was impossible as she was as strong as a wild mare. She caught him in a great bear-hug that almost cracked his spine. Grunting, twisting, he broke her hold and then wrestled in earnest. There, under the hot sun, before the glassy dead eyes of the bear, they wrestled.

Atalanta was a powerful fighter because she had been adopted by the she-bear, raised in the bear's cave, and treated like a cub. She had grown up among successive litters of bear cubs, wrestling with them, hunting with them; she had grown into a gloriously tanned, supple, fleet-footed young woman, strong as a she-bear herself. Wrestling Meleager seemed an easy matter to her. She planned to crush him in her hug and hurl him over the cliff.

However, as she wrestled with Meleager under the hot sun among the fragrance of thyme and crushed grass, something new happened. She had been used to wrestling shaggy bears, noticing with wonder how smooth her own arms and legs seemed against their mass of fur. She had wondered why she was so different, so hairless, and yet glad somehow that she was different. And now, as she held the young man in her mighty clutch, she felt his smoothness; and it was as though she were touching herself for the first time. Her own body seemed strange to her, yet deeply familiar. As she struggled, she found she could no longer know where his body ended and hers began. When she realized this, it seemed to her that the fragrance of the crushed grass rose like a sweet fog, making her dizzy. She found her knees buckling. She who could run miles up the steep slope of a mountain, outrunning even the mountain goats, felt her legs weakening. Her last thought, as her mind swooped and darkened was, "It's magic. He's doing some magic. He's fighting me with magic."

When her head cleared, she found they were sitting with their backs against a twisted olive tree near the edge of the cliff and looking out onto a great gulf of blueness where a brown eagle turned. Their arms were still about each other as if they were wrestling, but their bodies were still. She was telling him her name.

"I am Atalanta. I belong to this mountain, to the clan of mountain bears."

"I am Meleager," he said. "I belong to Atalanta."

So Meleager found the huntress he had dreamed of; they hunted together on hill and lowland, in forest and swamp and field, on foot and horseback, with dogs, or with long-legged hunting cats brought over from Egypt called Cheetahs, but more often, by themselves. They hunted so happily together and brought back so much game that word came to Artemis, Goddess of the Chase, Lady of the Wild Things; word came of Meleager, the handsome prince, the great spearman, and of his companion Atalanta, so tall and fleet and strong that people were saying she was Artemis herself come to earth. The goddess grew very angry.

"I'll show them there is only one Artemis," she cried. "I will set them a hunt they will never forget."

She dug her hands into the muck of the river Scamander and molded a huge boar, mud-colored, with evil red eyes. Far larger than any boar seen by man, large as a rhinoceros, armed with tusks, so long, heavy, and sharp he could shear down a tree with a toss of his head. She made this huge beast, filled him with a raging blood-thirst, and set him in Calydon to ravage the countryside.

THE HUNT

Immediately the beast began to spread death and terror throughout the land. He uprooted crops, killed horses, cattle, goats — and also those who tended them. He attacked men working in the fields, goring and trampling them into bloody rags. And, in a rage, the beast charged a farmhouse, knocking it over, and rooted among the rubble, killing those who had not been crushed by the falling beams. Shepherds and goatherds refused to graze their flocks on the hills; farmers feared to harvest their crops. The king, Meleager's father, was desperate. He asked his son's advice. Meleager was mad with excitement. He swore to his father that he would kill the boar.

"Just I, myself, and one companion. We can do it, father. No beast can escape us."

But the king said: "No, my son. This is no ordinary beast. It is too large, too irresistibly strong. It is a curse sent by some god whom we have unwittingly offended. Yet I have sacrificed to all the gods, and still the beast roams my poor country, destroying, killing . . ."

"I must hunt him, father! It is the quarry we have dreamed of — something worthy of our skill."

"I forbid it. You are my only son. If you are killed, the country will fall into the hands of your mother's foolish brothers. What we must do, Meleager, is invite all the heroes of Greece to hunt the beast. It will be a famous affair."

Thereupon messages were sent to all the heroes of Hellas, inviting them to Calydon to hunt the giant boar. They all accepted the invitation, kings, princes, and fierce soldiers of fortune who later sailed with Jason and fought at Troy.

However, the old king was not altogether pleased to be playing host to so many great men.

"I shall not be able to join the hunt," he said to his wife. "Meleager will have to do the honors while I stay home and guard the castle."

"Is that necessary?" said the queen. "Don't you trust your neighbors?"

"Yes, I trust them to act like themselves. These neighbors of ours didn't become so rich in land and cattle by right of purchase, my dear. They are men who have always taken what they wanted; this is how they have gained their property and their reputation. Frankly, I fear them more than I do the boar, and yet my heart tells me that my son may die on this hunt and that I should ride with him. I don't know what to do."

"You need not fear for our son," said Queen Althaea. "The Fates have made me the guardian of his life. Look . . ."

She unlocked the chest, showed him the charred brand of wood, and told him how she had been visited by Atropos, Lady of the Shears, who had promised that the prince would live while the brand remained unburned.

"So you may set your mind at rest, dear husband, and let him lead the hunt while you stay home and guard the castle. Besides, I am sending my two brothers to keep an eye on him. No, don't frown. I know your opinion of my brothers, but they are less lenient than you about certain matters. They will prevent him from bringing that wild girl of his to join the hunt."

"It is a mistake to interfere," said the king. "He loves that girl and will never love another."

"He shall not have her!" cried Althaea. "While I draw a breath he shall never bring her home as his wife."

"Well, I can't worry about her at the moment," said the king. "I have more important things on my mind. Fearsome beasts, fearsome guests — the wild girl will have to wait."

"She will wait long before she marries my son," said Althaea.

The next morning, everyone assembled for the hunt. The heroes were amazed when their host, Meleager, rode up with Atalanta at his side They gazed dumbfounded at the lovely, lithe young huntress, clad in a wolfskin tunic, bow and quiver slung, holding a javelin. A murmur rose. All were surprised; some of them were angry; a few of the younger ones were inflamed by her beauty and grew jealous of Meleager. The prince's solemn uncles rode toward him, beards bristling with outrage.

"It's a disgrace," they said. "You are bringing dishonor on yourself and on your noble guests. They do not wish to ride with this bear's-whelp from the hills."

Meleager thrust his horse between them and grasped their arms, squeezing them until they felt their elbows cracking in his iron hands.

"Listen to me," he whispered. "One more word out of you, and I will call off this hunt, send our guests home, and Atalanta and I will hunt the boar alone, as we have always wanted to do. But first I will smash your heads together just to show our guests where the fault lies."

The uncles said no more. Meleager sounded a call upon his horn that rang through the hills, and the glittering company rode out to find the boar.

They did not have far to ride. Their quarry came to meet them, taking up its position as wisely as a general disposing troops; it came to earth in a canyon where the walls narrowed so that it could be attacked only from the front, and by only two men at a time. This rocky bottle-neck was overgrown with willows, and the boar crouched in there unseen, waiting for the hunters.

However, the hunters were old hands at this. They did not rush in to attack him, but strung themselves out before the entrance to his lair, shouting, clashing spear on shield, trying to taunt him into the open. They succeeded only too well, not knowing his size and speed. The boar came hurtling out of the willow brush with the crashing force of a huge boulder falling down a mountainside. He ploughed into a party of hunters, knocking them in all directions, whirling his huge bulk lightly as a fox, and cutting two of the men to shreds under his razor-sharp hooves. He charged again at the fleeing hunters, lunging at one with his tusks, and shearing his leg off at the hip.

The two warrior brothers, Telamon and Peleus, who became the father of Achilles, showed their great courage by walking slowly in on the boar, spears out-thrust. Their attack inspired two of the others, Ancaeus and Eurytion, to walk in behind the boar from opposite sides. But the beast broke out of the circle of spears by charging Telamon. Peleus flung his spear; it grazed the boar's shoulder, was deflected, and pierced Eurytion, who fell dead. Now Ancaeus, swinging his battle-ax at the boar, had his thrust parried by a sweep of one tusk; and then with a counter-thrust the boar ripped out the man's belly, gutting him as a fisherman does a fish. The beast then whirled and charged Peleus, who might have died on the spot, leaving no son named Achilles (and Hector might have gone unslain, and Troy, perhaps, might have stood unburned), but Atalanta drew her bow and sent a shaft into the vulnerable spot behind the boar's ear. It sank in up to the feathers. Another beast would have been killed instantly, but the boar still lived and remained murderously strong.

Screaming with pain the boar chased Atalanta. Theseus rose from behind a rock and flung a javelin, he missed. Atalanta swiftly notched another arrow and stood facing the boar under his shoulder, turning him from his charge enough for her to send the shaft into his eye.

But Meleager, shouting a wild war-cry, flung himself in the boar's path, hurling a javelin as he ran. It went into the boar under his shoulder, turning him from his charge toward Meleager, who kept running, and leaped clear over the charging beast like a Cretan bull-dancer. He came down on the other side, and before the animal could turn, thrust his sword under the great hump of muscle, cutting the spinal cord and breaking the cable of hot life; the boar fell dead.

Meleager pulled out his sword, and then calmly as though on a stag-hunt, knelt at the side of the giant beast and skinned him. He walked to Atalanta with the bloody pelt in his arms, bowed, and offered it to her, saying, "Your arrow struck him first. The pelt belongs to you."

Now this boarhide was a most valuable present. It was so thick and tough that it made a wonderful flexible war vest, lighter and stronger than armor, able to turn spear-thrust and flying arrow. There was much resentment when Meleager gave the hide to the girl; the uncles, seeing this resentment, reproached Meleager again, accusing him of favoritism and inhospitality. The elder uncle, Plexippus, began to curse Atalanta, calling her by filthy names; his brother echoed him.

Meleager wiped the blood from his sword and carefully dried it with a handful of rushes. He inspected the gleaming blade, and then swung it twice; the heads of his uncles rolled in the dust so swiftly severed that they still seemed to be cursing as they fell. Then Meleager said, "I beg you, sirs, pardon this unseemly family brawl; but if any one of you feels too much offended, I shall be glad to measure swords with him. If not, you are all invited to the castle, to a feast celebrating the death of the boar, and honoring his fair executioner, the huntress, Atalanta, whom I intend to make my wife."

The heroes raised a great shout. Many of them were still angry, others jealous, but they all admired courage when they saw it; besides they had had enough fighting for the day so they rode back to the castle, and Atalanta and Meleager rode off to be alone for a few hours before the feast.

When the hunters returned to the castle, they were met by the king and queen who eagerly demanded to hear their tale. But when they were told of the dispute over the hide and of how Meleager had killed his uncles and presented Atalanta to the company as his bride, the queen grew white with fury and rushed to her room.

There she sank to her knees on the stone floor and cried, "Bad prince, disobedient son, you have dispatched my two brothers to Tartarus, and in their noble stead propose to bring home this wild nameless nymph of the hills. This shall not be, my son, my enemy. The Fates have given your mother the power to end your evil ways . . ."

Mad with grief, Althaea sprang to the chest, flung it open, pulled the charred stick from its hiding place, and threw it on the fire. She watched it burn.

At this time Meleager and Atalanta were in their favorite place under the twisted olive tree on the cliff, looking out into the great blue gulf of space and speaking softly.

"I want to be your wife," said Atalanta. "You are the only one I shall ever love, but why must we live in a castle? Why must I be a queen, and wear dresses, and sit on a throne? Why can't we stay as we are, roaming the hills, hunting, fighting?"

"We will, we will!" cried Meleager. "For every day we spend indoors being king and queen and making laws and such, for each day spent so poorly, we will spend ten days riding, hunting, fighting, you and I together side by side. I promise you, Atalanta. And this I promise too . . ."

He stopped. She saw him clutch at his chest, saw his eyes bulge, his face blacken. She caught him in her arms. His head snapped back; his scorched lips parted. He uttered a strangling howl of agony; his head lolled, and he was dead.

In the castle, Queen Althaea prodded the fire with her toe, scattering the last ashes. Then she straightened her robes and went down to tend to her guests.

THE RACE

After Meleager's death, Calydon became hateful to Atalanta. She left its familiar crags and slopes, and made her way to Arcadia. Obeying some dim instinct, a dumb homeward impulse that was the only thing she felt in her terrible grief, she went back to Arcadia where she had been born.

The king, her father, now very old, realized from her story that she was his daughter, whom, as an infant, he had exposed on the mountain . . . and that she had grown up to be as mighty a hunter and warrior as any son he could have hoped for. He recognized her as his child, and she lived in the castle.

But hunting and everything that reminded her of her murdered lover was hateful to Atalanta now. Her fame had spread throughout the land, and the heroes who had gone on the Calydonian Hunt, and others too, came to woo the warrior-maiden for she was an orphan no more, but a princess, who would inherit land and cattle and gold. So they came acourting.

Atalanta could not bear the sight of them. "I will never marry another," she said to her father. "That part of me died with Meleager. I will never love another man. Send them away."

"I cannot insult them," said her father. "They are too powerful. If I seek to drive them away, they will make war upon me, conquer me; and you will be dragged off, a captive instead of a wife."

"Whoever takes me captive won't live long enough to enjoy it," said Atalanta. "However, let us do this: announce to them that I will marry only the man who can outrun me in a foot race. If he wins, he marries me; if he loses, he loses his head."

The king agreed. Atalanta's terms were announced. Most of the heroes who had watched her in action on the hunt, had observed her speed of movement, and had studied her long legs, knew what the outcome of a race must be, and decided to seek brides elsewhere. But some of the younger men were rash enough to persist. One by one, they raced Atalanta. The entire court turned out to see these races. Race followed race; she wanted no rest in between, and it seemed to the spectators that the young men still scrambled at the starting post as Atalanta flashed across the finish line.

She was merciless about imposing the penalty. Each losing suitor walked to the chopping block and paid with his head. Now, there was one young man, Hippomenes, who had also been at the Calydonian Hunt, although he had played no great role there. But he had fallen violently in love with Atalanta, so much in love that he was grieved at the death of Meleager because he knew that it would pain her so. Without ever being bold enough to make himself known to her, he had followed her at a distance, trailing her from Calydon to Arcadia and taking up residence there. He planned each day so that he would get a glimpse of her and this was enough to carry him to the next day. Still she had never met him.

When the races were announced, Hippomenes experienced a curious mixture of feelings. He was happy, on the one hand, that she was showing her scorn of other suitors; sad, on the other hand, because he realized that her scorn would extend to himself, if she knew him. He went each day to watch the races and again felt confused for he became each young man in the race and felt death crawl in his veins as he saw her flash across the finish line. He was each young man who laid his head on the bloody block, yet he was glad when the head rolled because there was one more rival gone. And through it all ran a curious thread of bitter joy, for his torment, he knew, had to end soon. The race would give him the chance to pay for this terrible love with his life.

When all the suitors had been beheaded, he announced himself as an entry. Everyone pleaded with him not to run. He was a gentle young man, with a soft voice and an easy smile. He did not look much like anyone's idea of a hero, and no one believed he had a chance. Even cruel

Atalanta said, "Don't be a fool. Go lose your head over some other girl. I'm not for you."

But for all his gentleness, he could not be moved. He insisted so the race was set. Now, all the other young men who had raced Atalanta had prayed to various gods to give them victory: to Hermes, the wing-footed, god of games; to Ares, god of victories; to Artemis, mistress of the chase. They prayed to Athene for strategy, to Zeus, for strength. But Hippomenes prayed to none of these. He thought to himself, "the others want to coerce her. I want her to want me." . . . So he prayed to Aphrodite, goddess of love.

Aphrodite appeared to him when he was asleep, gave him three golden apples, and told him how to use them. When he awoke he knew that he had been dreaming, but there were the three golden apples gleaming on his bed. He hid them in his tunic and went out to race.

It was a brilliant sunny day; all the court was there. Atalanta had never appeared more beautiful than she looked that day walking to the starting post in her short white tunic, her long dark hair falling free. Hippomenes smiled at her and wished her good morning, holding tight to the slippery golden apples under his tunic so that they would not roll away before the race began. She received his greeting, and nodded, gravely. Then she studied him, frowning. Why was he clutching at his clothes in that odd way? That was no way to hold yourself before a race.

She felt a strange, hot lump form at the base of her throat; something about his hands, something terrible about the pose of those hands grasping at his tunic. Then she remembered, remembered the way her beloved Meleager had clutched at his belly when the curse was burning in him, just before he died in her arms.

She was so sunk in memory that she did not hear the trumpet call, starting the race, and Hippomenes was far in the lead when she woke up and began to run. He heard her light footfalls behind him, heard the easy music of her breathing. Then a great shout from the crowd, and he knew that she had closed the gap. He let one of the golden apples slip away and roll across her path.

And Atalanta, still remembering, running in a dream, saw the golden flash and automatically stooped to scoop up the rolling apple. She loped along slowly as she examined the glittering thing. She saw her face in it, distorted, made gross, and she thought, "That's how I will look when I am old . . ."

Then she heard the crowd shout, raised her head, and saw Hippomenes far in the lead. She darkened her mind, and let the speed surge through her legs and into her drumming feet until she was running just behind him again.

"Poor boy," she thought. "Am I tormenting him with hope? Or is such torture love's gift too? Would it have been better never to have seen Meleager, never to have loved him, never to have suffered by losing him? No! Worse, worse, worse!"

Just then Hippomenes dropped the second apple. It rolled, flashing.

"What a pretty thing," she thought. "Like one of Aphrodite's apples from that magic tree in the Hesperides. I will take it and the other one and bring them both to Calydon, to Meleager's grave."

Now Hippomenes had thrown this apple harder; it had rolled quite a way before she decided to go back for it. When she had picked it up, she saw Hippomenes far up the track, almost at the finish line. She ran with desperate speed then and caught him just two steps before the end.

He dropped the third apple. She laughed with scorn. "The fool . . . does he think I'll stop for that one and let him win? I'll simply cross the finish line and come back for the apple while he's being led to the block."

The apple lay before her feet. It was not rolling. All she had to do was bend in her course and scoop it up. But did she have time? The apple burned. It became a head bright with blood. Hippomenes' head falling under the ax. It changed into the head of Meleager's uncle being scythed off by the flashing sword . . . became Meleager's face bright with sweat and agony . . . became her own face, reflected, gross, distorted, old . . . growing now, swelling, blown up by the roaring of the crowd, mushrooming into the golden radiance of the sun — so enormous, so indifferently hot — touching the earth with seasons, budding flowers, beasts, hunters, nymphs, horses, amorous princes, angry queens . . . birth and murder . . .

She held the three golden apples, dreaming into their polished fire, her face wet with tears, and the roaring of the crowd was dim, lost thunder, like the pounding of the surf. She stood there on the course, lost in her dream, as Hippomenes crossed the finish line and came back to claim his prize.

MIDAS

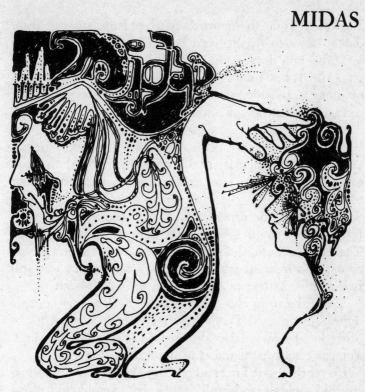

There was a king named Midas, and what he loved best in the world was gold. He had plenty of his own, but he could not bear the thought of anyone else having any. Each morning he awoke very early to watch the sunrise and said, "Of all the gods, if gods there be, I like you least, Apollo. How dare you ride so unthriftily in your sun-chariot scattering golden sheaves of light on rich and poor alike — on king and peasant, on merchant, shepherd, warrior? This is an evil thing, oh wastrel god, for only kings should have gold; only the rich know what to do with it."

After a while these words of complaint, uttered each dawn, came to Apollo, and he was angry. He appeared to Midas in a dream and said, "Other gods would punish you, Midas, but I am famous for my even temper. Instead of doing you violence, I will show you how gracious I can be by granting you a wish. What is it to be?"

Midas cried, "Let everything I touch turn to gold!"

He shouted this out of his sleep in a strangling greedy voice, and the guards in the doorway nodded to each other and said, "The king calls out. He must be dreaming of gold again."

Wearied by the dream, Midas slept past sunrise; when he awoke it was full morning. He went out into his garden. The sun was high, the sky was blue. A soft breeze played among the trees. It was a glorious morning. He was still half asleep. Tatters of the dream were in his head.

"Can it be true?" he said to himself. "They say the gods appear in dreams. That's how men know them. On the other hand I know that dreams are false, teasing things. You can't believe them. Let us put it to the test."

He reached out his hand and touched a rose. It turned to gold — petals and stalk, it turned to gold and stood there rigid, heavy, gleaming. A bee buzzed out of its stiff folds, furious; it lit on Midas' hand to sting him. The king looked at the heavy golden bee on the back of his hand and moved it to his finger.

"I shall wear it as a ring," he said.

Midas went about touching all his roses, seeing them stiffen and gleam. They lost their odor. The disappointed bees rose in swarms and buzzed angrily away. Butterflies departed. The hard flowers tinkled like little bells when the breeze moved among them, and the king was well pleased.

His little daughter, the princess, who had been playing in the garden, ran to him and said, "Father, father, what has happened to the roses?"

"Are they not pretty, my dear?"

"No! They're ugly! They're horrid and sharp and I can't smell them any more. What happened?"

"A magical thing."

"Who did the magic?"

"I did."

"Unmagic it, then! I hate these roses."

She began to cry.

"Don't cry," he said, stroking her head. "Stop crying, and I will give you a golden doll with a gold-leaf dress and tiny golden shoes."

She stopped crying. He felt the hair grow spiky under his fingers. Her eyes stiffened and froze into place. The little blue vein in her neck stopped pulsing. She was a statue, a figure of pale gold standing in the garden path with lifted face. Her tears were tiny golden beads on her golden cheeks. He looked at her and said, "This is unfortunate. I'm sorry it happened. I have no time to be sad this morning. I shall be busy turning things into gold. But, when I have a moment, I shall think about this problem; I promise." He hurried out of the garden which had become unpleasant to him.

On Midas' way back to the castle he amused himself by kicking up gravel in the path and watching it tinkle down as tiny nuggets. The door he opened became golden; the chair he sat upon became solid gold like his throne. The plates turned into gold, and the cups became gold cups before the amazed eyes of the servants, whom he was careful not to touch. He wanted them to continue being able to serve him; he was very hungry.

With great relish Midas picked up a piece of bread and honey. His teeth bit metal; his mouth was full of metal. He felt himself choking. He reached into his mouth and pulled out a golden slab of bread, all bloody now, and flung it through the window. Very lightly now he touched the other food to see what would happen. Meat . . . apples . . . walnuts . . . they all turned to gold even when he touched them with only the tip of his finger . . . and when he did not touch them with his fingers, when he lifted them on his fork, they became gold as soon as they touched his lips, and he had to put them back onto the plate. He was savagely hungry. Worse than hunger, when he thought about drinking, he realized that wine, or water, or milk would turn to gold in his mouth and choke him if he drank. As he thought that he could not drink, thirst began to burn in his belly. He felt himself full of hot dry sand, felt that the lining of his head was on fire.

"What good is all my gold?" he cried, "if I cannot eat and cannot drink?"

He shrieked with rage, pounded on the table, and flung the plates about. All the servants ran from the room in fright. Then Midas raced out of the castle, across the bridge that spanned the moat, along the golden gravel path into the garden where the stiff flowers chimed hatefully, and the statue of his daughter looked at him with scooped and empty eyes. There in the garden, in the blaze of the sun, he raised his arms heavenward, and cried, "You, Apollo, false god, traitor! You pretended to forgive me, but you punished me with a gift!"

Then it seemed to him that the sun grew brighter, that the light thickened, that the sun-god stood before him in the path, tall, stern, clad in burning gold. A voice said, "On your knees, wretch!"

He fell to his knees.

"Do you repent?"

"I repent. I will never desire gold again. I will never accuse the gods. Pray, revoke the fatal wish."

Apollo reached his hand and touched the roses. The tinkling stopped, they softened, swayed, blushed. Fragrance grew on the air. The bees returned, and the butterflies. He touched the statue's cheek. She lost her stiffness, her metallic gleam. She ran to the roses, knelt among them, and cried, "Oh, thank you, father. You've changed them back again." Then she ran off, shouting and laughing.

Apollo said, "I take back my gift. I remove the golden taint from your touch, but you are not to escape without punishment. Because you have been the most foolish of men, you shall wear always a pair of donkey's ears."

Midas touched his ears. They were long and furry. He said, "I thank you for your forgiveness, Apollo . . . even though it comes with a punishment."

"Go now," said Apollo. "Eat and drink. Enjoy the roses. Watch your child grow. Life is the only wealth, man. In your great thrift, you have been wasteful of life, and that is the sign you wear on your head. Farewell."

Midas put a tall pointed hat on his head so that no one would see his ears. Then he went in to eat and drink his fill.

For years he wore the cap so that that no one would know of his disgrace. But the servant who cut his hair had to know so Midas swore him to secrecy, warning that it would cost him his head if he spoke of the king's ears. But the servant who was a coward was also a gossip. He could not bear to keep a secret, especially a secret so mischievous. Although he was afraid to tell it, he felt that he would burst if he didn't.

One night he went out to the banks of the river, dug a little hole, put his mouth to it, and whispered, "Midas has donkey's ears, Midas has donkey's ears . . ." and quickly filled up the hole again, and ran back to the castle, feeling better.

But the river-reeds heard him, and they always whisper to each other when the wind seethes among them. They were heard whispering, "Midas has donkey's ears . . . donkey's ears . . .", and soon the whole country was whispering, "Have you heard about Midas? Have you heard about his ears?"

When the king heard, he knew who had told the secret and ordered the man's head cut off; but then he thought, "The god forgave me, perhaps I had better forgive this blabbermouth." Therefore he let the treacherous man keep his head.

Then Apollo appeared again and said, "Midas, you have learned the final lesson, mercy. As you have done, so shall you be done by."

And Midas felt his long hairy ears dwindling back to normal.

He was an old man now. His daughter, the princess, was grown. He had grandchildren. Sometimes he tells his smallest granddaughter the story of how her mother was turned into a golden statue, and he says, "See, I'm changing you too. Look, your hair is all gold."

And she pretends to be frightened.

The women of Cyprus were displeased with Pygmalion. He was one of the few unmarried young men on the island, and it seemed that he meant to stay that way. He was a sculptor who lived alone in a house he had knocked together out of an old stable, one enormous room on a hill overlooking the sea, far away from any neighbor. Here he spent the days very happily. Great unhewn blocks of marble stood about, and tubs of clay, and a crowd of figures, men and women, nymphs, satyrs, wolves, lions, bulls, and dolphins. Some of them were half-carved, some of them clay daubs, almost shapeless; and others were finished statues, marvelous gleaming shapes of white marble.

Sometimes people came and bought Pygmalion's figures. He sold only those he was tired of looking at, but would never set a price. He took anything offered. Often, he would give his work away, if he thought that someone enjoyed looking at it and had no money to pay. He ate when he was hungry, slept when he was tired, worked when he felt like it, swam in the sea when hot, and spent days without seeing anyone.

"Oh, I have plenty of company," he'd say. "Plenty of statues around, you know. Not very good conversationalists, but they listen beautifully."

Now, all this irritated the mothers and daughters of Cyprus exceedingly. A bachelor is bad enough, a happy bachelor is intolerable. And so they were resolved that he should marry.

"He's earning enough to keep a wife . . . or he would be if he charged properly. That's another reason he needs one. My Althea is a very shrewd girl. She'd see he got the right prices for his work . . ."

"My Laurel is an excellent housekeeper. She'd clean out that pig-sty of his, and make it fit to live in . . ."

"My daughter has very strict ideas. She'd make him toe the mark. Where does he get the models for those nymph statues? Tell me that? Who knows what goes on in that stable of his? . ."

"*My* daughter . . ."

And so it went. They talked like this all the time, and Pygmalion was very much aware of their plans for him. More than ever he resolved to keep himself to himself.

Now Cyprus was an island sacred to Aphrodite, for it was the first land she touched when she arose from the sea.

The mothers of the island decided to use her favor for their own purposes. They crowded into the temple of Aphrodite and recited this prayer:

"Oh, great goddess of Love, you who rose naked and dripping from the sea and walked upon this shore, making it blossom with trees and flowers, you, Aphrodite, hear our plea: touch the heart of young Pygmalion, who has become as hard as his own marble. Weave your amorous spell, plaiting it into the tresses of one of our maidens, making it a snare for his wild loneliness. Bid your son, the Archer of Love, plant one of his arrows in that indifferent young man so that he becomes infected with a sweet sickness for which there is only one cure. Please, goddess, forbid him all solitary joy. Bind him to one of our maidens. Make him love her and take her as his wife."

That night Pygmalion, dreaming, was visited by the goddess who said, "Pygmalion, I have been asked to marry you off. Do you have any preferences?"

Pygmalion, being an artist, was acquainted with the terrible reality of dreams and knew that the matter was serious, that he was being threatened. He said, "There is one lady I fancy. But she is already married."

"Who?"

"You."

"Me?"

"You, Aphrodite, queen of beauty, lady of delight. How can you think that I who in my daily work will accept nothing less than the forms of ideal beauty, how can you think that I could pin my highest aspiration on any but the most perfect face and form? Yours, Aphrodite. Yours, yours. I love you, and you alone. And until I can find a mortal maid of the same perfection, I will not love."

Now, Aphrodite, although a goddess, was also a woman. In fact, her divinity was precisely this, womanliness raised to its highest power. She was much pleased by this ardent praise. She knelt beside Pygmalion and, stroking his face, said, "Truly, you are a fair-spoken young man. I find your arguments very persuasive. But what am I to do? I have promised the mothers of Cyprus that you shall wed, and I must not break my promise."

"Did you tell them *when?*"

"No, I set no time."

"Then grant me this: permit me to remain unwed until I do one more statue. It will be my masterwork, the thing I have been training myself for. Let me do it now, and allow me to remain unmarried until I complete it for the vision is upon me, goddess. The time has come. I must do this last figure."

"Of whom?"

"Of you, of course! Of you, of you! I told you that I have loved you all my life without ever having seen you. And now that you have appeared to me, now that I do see you, why then I must carve you in marble. It is simple. This is what my life is for; it is my way of loving you, a way that you cannot deny me."

"I see . . . And how long will this work take?"

"Until it is finished. What else can I say? If you will be good enough to visit me like this whenever you can spare the time, I will fill my eyes with you and work on your image alone, putting all else aside. Once and for all I shall be able to cast in hard cold marble the flimsy, burning dream of man, his dream of beauty, his dream of you . . ."

"Very well," said Aphrodite, "you may postpone your marriage until my statue is completed." She smiled at him. "And every now and again I shall come to pose."

Pygmalion worked first in clay. He took it between his hands and thought of Aphrodite — of her round arms, of the strong column of her neck, of her long, full thighs, of the smooth swimming of her back muscles when she turned from the waist — and his hands followed his thinking, pressing the clay to the shape of her body. She came to him at night, sliding in and out of his dreams, telling him stories about herself. He used a whole tub-full of clay making a hundred little Aphrodites, each in a different pose. He caught her at that moment when she emerged from the sea, shaking back her wet hair, lifting her face to the sky which she saw for the first time. He molded her in the Hall of the Gods receiving marriage offers, listening to Poseidon, and Hermes, and Apollo press their claims, head tilted, shoulders straight, smiling to herself, pleasing everyone, but refusing to answer. He molded her in full magnificent fury, punishing Narcissus, kneeling on the grass, teasing the shy Adonis, and then mourning him, slain.

He caught her in a hundred poses, then stood the little clay figures about, studying them, trying to mold them in his mind to a total image that he could carve in marble. He had planned to work slowly. After all, the whole thing was a trick of his to postpone marriage; but as he made the lovely little dolls and posed them among her adventures, his hands took on a schedule of their own. The dream invaded daylight, and he found himself working with wild fury.

When the clay figures were done, he was ready for marble. He set the heavy mass of polished stone in the center of the room and arranged his clay studies about it. Then he took mallet and chisel, and began to work—

it was as if the cold tools became living parts of himself. The chisel was like his own finger, with a sharp fingernail edge; the mallet was his other hand, curled into a fist. With these living tools he reached into the marble and worked the stone as if it were clay, chopping, stroking, carving, polishing. And from the stone a body began to rise as Aphrodite had risen from the white foam of the sea.

He never knew when he had finished. He had not eaten for three days. His brain was on fire, his hands flying. He had finished carving; he was polishing the marble girl now with delicate files. Then, suddenly, he knew that it was finished. His head felt full of ashes; his hands hung like lumps of meat. He fell onto his pallet and was drowned in sleep.

He awoke in the middle of the night. The goddess was standing near his bed, he saw. Had she come to pose for him again? It was too late. Then he saw that it was not Aphrodite, but the marble figure standing in the center of the room, the white marble gathering all the moonlight to her. She shone in the darkness, looking as though she were trying to leap from the pediment.

He went to the statue and tried to find something unfinished, a spot he could work on. But there was nothing. She was complete. Perfect. A masterwork. Every line of her drawn taut by his own strength stretched to the breaking point, the curvings of her richly rounded with all the love he had never given to a human being. There she was, an image of Aphrodite. But not Aphrodite. She was herself, a marble girl, modeled after the goddess, but different; younger; human.

"You are Galatea," he said. "That is your name."

He went to a carved wooden box and took out jewels that had belonged to his mother. He decked Galatea in sapphires and diamonds. Then he sat at the foot of the statue, looking at it, until the sun came up. The birds sang, a donkey brayed; he heard the shouting of children, the barking of dogs. He sat there, looking at her. All that day he sat, and all that night. Still he had not eaten. And now it seemed that all the other marble figures in the room were swaying closer, were shadows crowding about, threatening him.

She did not move. She stood there, tall, radiant. His mother's jewels sparkled on her throat and on her arms. Her marble foot spurned the pediment.

Then Aphrodite herself stepped into the room. She said, "I have come to make you keep your promise, Pygmalion. You have finished the statue. You must marry."

"Whom?"

"Whomever you choose. Do you not wish to select your own bride?"

"Yes."

"Then choose. Choose any girl you like. Whoever she is, whatever she is, she shall love you. For I am pleased with the image you have made of me. Choose."

"I choose — her," said Pygmalion, pointing to the statue.

"You may not."

"Why not?"

"She does not live. She is a statue."

"My statues will outlive all who are living now," said Pygmalion.

"That is just a way of speaking. She is not flesh and blood; she is a marble image. You must choose a living girl."

"I must choose where I love. I love her who is made in your image, goddess."

"It cannot be."

"You said, 'whoever she is, whatever she is . . . .'"

"Yes, but I did not mean a statue."

"I did. You call her lifeless, but I say my blood went into her making. My bones shaped hers. My fingers loved her surfaces. I polished her with all my knowledge, all my wit. She has seen all my strength, all my weakness, she has watched me sleep, played with my dreams. We *are* wed, Aphrodite, in a fatal incomplete way. Please, dear goddess, give her to me."

"Impossible."

"You are a goddess. Nothing is impossible."

"I am the Goddess of Love. There is no love without life."

"There is no life without love. I know how you can do it. Look . . . I stand here. I place my arm about her; my face against hers. Now, use your power, turn me to marble too. We shall be frozen together in this moment of time, embracing each other through eternity. This will suffice. For I tell you that without her my brain is ash, my hands are meat; I do not wish to breathe, to see, to be."

Aphrodite, despite herself, was warmed by his pleas. After all, he had made the statue in her image. It was pleasing to know that her beauty, even cast in lifeless marble, could still drive a young man mad.

"You are mad," she said. "Quite mad. But in people like you, I suppose, it is called inspiration. Very well, young sir, put your arms about her again.

Pygmalion embraced the cold marble. He kissed the beautiful stiff lips. and then he felt the stone flush with warmth. He felt the hard polished marble turn to warm silky flesh. He felt the mouth grow warm and move against his. He felt arms come up and hug him tight. He was holding a live girl in his arms.

He stepped off the pediment, holding her hand. She stepped after him. They fell on their knees before Aphrodite and thanked her for her gift.

"Rise, beautiful ones," she said. "It is the morning of love. Go to my temple, adorn it with garlands. You, Pygmalion, set about the altar those clever little dolls of me you have made. Thank me loudly for my blessings for I fear the mothers of Cyprus will not be singing my praises so ardently for some time."

She left. Galatea looked about the great dusty studio, littered with tools, scraps of marble, and spillings of clay. She looked at Pygmalion — tousled, unshaven, with bloodshot eyes and stained tunic — and said, "Now, dear husband, it's my turn to work on you."

AFTERWORD

In Greek mythology, heroes and monsters alike are spawned by the gods. The Gorgons are granddaughters of Rhea, mother of Zeus, which makes them cousins of their arch-enemy, Perseus. In other words, both good and evil come from the gods. Good is the divine energy expressing itself through men of high deeds. Evil is the same energy, twisted. When hero confronts monster in these myths, there is apt to be a family quarrel.

This sophisticated pagan idea has influenced all the religions that came after.

The birth of the monster is attended by rage, and that is what makes him monstrous, the wrath of a god — or, more often, a goddess — carving a dangerous, ugly form for itself out of living flesh.

These tales are drenched in sunlight, and this sunlight is more than weather; it is a moral quality. Heroes love to cavort in the open air, to fly, to cleave the burning sea, to race on the hills, to hunt over the fields. But monsters belong to darkness. The Gorgons live where it is always winter. Cerberus, the three-headed dog, guards the gate of dark Tartarus. Scylla and Echidne, those dread serpent-women, lurk in a sea-cave waiting to make shipwrecks, to catch sailors and crack their bones. The Minotaur howls in a maze of shadows. All monsters wait in darkness; and when heroes hunt them, they must come in out of the sun. The ordeal starts right there.

So we see a great religious theme: the eternal struggle between the powers of Light and the powers of Darkness embodied in these simple stories in a way that has branded itself on man's consciousness forever.

ROMAN NAMES FOR GREEK GODS

The Romans had very little mythology of their own. They took over the Hellenic idea completely; but they did rename the Greek gods, and often the Latin names are better known. Here are both sets of names:

GREEK		ROMAN	
Zeus	King of Heaven, Ruler of the Gods.	Jupiter	Name derived from *Zeus-pater*, Father Zeus.
Hera	Queen of Heaven.	Juno	
Poseidon	God of the Sea.	Neptune	
Hades	God of the Under-world.	Pluto	Strictly speaking, not a Latin name but a Greek word meaning "rich"—a name chosen to flatter a dangerous god. It is in this mood that those fearsome flying crones, the Furies, Hades' helpers, were called the *Eumenides,* or Kindly Ones.
Athene	Goddess of Wisdom.	Minerva	
Artemis	Moon-goddess, Queen of the Chase.	Diane	
Apollo	The Sun-god.	Phoebus	Actually adapted from a Greek word meaning "bright."
Demeter	Mother of Crops.	Ceres	
Ares	God of War.	Mars	
Hermes	The Messenger-god, Patron of travelers, gamblers, thieves.	Mercury	
Hephaestus	The Smith-god.	Vulcan	
Cronos	Father of the Gods.	Saturn	
Rhea	Mother of the Gods.	Cybele	
Persephone	Queen of the Under-world.	Proserpina	
Hestia	Goddess of the Hearth.	Vesta	
Nemesis	Goddess of Luck and Vengeance.	Fortuna	

MYTHOLOGY BECOMES LANGUAGE

It is fascinating to see how the characters and events of these myths have become words and phrases which have entered the English language. Each word, when you know its ancestry, can become a percussion cap exploding the wonderful colored lights of a story in your head.

Aphrodisiac, a love-potion, was named for *Aphrodite,* Goddess of Love.

Atlas, a map, was named after the Titan who bore the sky on his shoulders and was turned to stone by Perseus.

Cloth is a plain little word with a very dramatic history. The Greeks believed that destiny was controlled by three terrible sisters called the Fates. Clotho spun the thread of life on her spindle; Lachesis measured the thread; and the most dangerous sister, Atropos, Lady of the Shears, snipped the thread of life when it had been measured out. Our word "cloth" comes from *Clotho,* the spinner.

Echo is derived from the name of the nymph, *Echo,* who fell in love with Narcissus (described on page 111). She could not tell him of her love because she was under a curse which allowed her to repeat only the last word of what was said to her.

Erotic, relating to love, is derived from *Eros,* Aphrodite's son, the secret archer, whose arrows were tipped with the sweet poison of love.

Fortune is a very common word that is derived from *Fortuna,* the Roman Goddess of Luck and Vengeance, Mistress of Destiny. Actually, her name was a variant of the Latin word, *vortumna,* meaning "turner," because she turned the giant wheel of the year, stopping it at either happiness, sorrow, life, or death.

Galatea, a biddable girl, was the name of the statue which Pygmalion carved to the shape of his heart's desire.

Icarian, meaning "of bold vaulting ambition," is derived from *Icarus,* son of Daedalus, who insisted on flying too near the sun and died doing it.

Junoesque, meaning stately, majestic, is a word used to describe women only and comes from *Juno,* the Roman Queen of Heaven, who was of imposing figure.

Labyrinth, a "maze," is derived from the name of the prison-garden full of puzzling paths, built by Daedalus at King Minos' command to confine the Minotaur. Actually, the Cretan word, *labys*, means ax; the double-headed ax was the royal symbol in Crete. The palace of the king at Knossos was known as "The Ax-House," and it was in the garden of this palace that Daedalus built his maze.

Martial, meaning warlike, comes from *Mars*, the Roman God of War.

Medusa-locks, meaning wild hair, is a phrase named after the hissing snake coiffure of the fearsome Gorgon sister, *Medusa*, whom Perseus killed.

Mercurial, meaning swift, unstable, changeable, refers to the disposition of *Mercury*, the Roman Messenger-god.

Midas-touch, the golden touch, is said of those who are good at making money.

Narcissistic means to be obsessed by the idea of one's own beauty. It is taken from *Narcissus*, the boy who fell in love with his own reflection in a stream and knelt there admiring it until he became rooted to the ground and was changed into a flower.

Neptune, the Roman God of the Sea, has given his name to countless restaurants and inns, especially those emphasizing sea food.

Orpheum refers to *Orpheus*, the sweetest singer to ever sing. This term is used by many theaters and places of entertainment.

Panic is derived from the god, *Pan*, the goat-footed, flute-playing king of field and wood whose war-cry was supposed to spread frenzy and fear among his enemies.

Procrustes-bed is a phrase meaning any difficult situation which cannot be changed but to which man must adapt himself. It comes from the uncomfortable hospitality offered by the innkeeper, *Procrustes*, who bolted guests to the bed. If they were too short, he stretched them; if too long, he chopped off their legs to fit. However, Theseus made him lie in his own bed.

Psyche is perhaps the most misused word in the language. In Greek it meant "soul" and was personified in myth by a beautiful princess, beloved of Eros himself, who lost her husband and her sense of herself through mistrust but regained both when she dropped her suspicions and took on the risks that love brings. In English, however, the word has come to mean the entire mental apparatus and has given birth to a host of mechanical words like psychotic, psychology, psycho-analysis, etc.

Pygmalion, the term applied to a man who can train a girl to be the way he wants, is derived from *Pygmalion*, the sculptor of Cyprus, who carved a statue in the shape of his heart's desire.

Saturday is named after the god, Saturn, a Roman name for Cronos.

Terpsichorean, relating to the dance, is derived from the Muse, *Terpsichore*, who presided over dance.

Typhoon, a violent wind, comes from *Typhon*, a terrible monster. He was half donkey, half serpent; he had great leathery wings and flew through the air shrieking horribly, spitting flames.

Vestal means nun-like. The term is derived from *Vesta*, the Roman Goddess of the Hearth. In ancient Rome, maidens were consecrated to the service of this goddess; their duty was to keep the sacred flame burning upon her altar night and day. They lived in her temple always and never married.

Volcano is derived from *Vulcan*, the Roman Smith-god, who took a mountain as his smithy. When he heated up his forge, clouds of smoke arose from the mountain.

BIBLIOGRAPHY FOR
SUPPLEMENTARY READING

Asimov, Isaac. *Words from the Myths*. Houghton Mifflin: Boston, 1961.

Bulfinch, Thomas. *Bulfinch's Mythology*. Thomas Y. Crowell: New York (no date).

Grant, Michael. *Myths of the Greeks and Romans*. World Publishers: New York, 1962.

Graves, Robert. *The Greek Myths*. Penguin Books: Baltimore, 1955.

Hamilton, Edith. *Mythology*. New American Library: New York, 1940.

Hamilton, Edith. *The Greek Way to Western Civilization*. New American Library: New York, 1948.

Hays, H. R. *In The Beginnings*. G. P. Putnam's Sons: New York, 1963.

Rose, H. J. *A Handbook of Greek Mythology*. E. P. Dutton: New York, 1959.

Schwab, Gustav. *Gods and Heroes: Myths and Epics of Ancient Greece*. Fawcett World Library: New York, 1965.

Updike, John. *The Centaur*. Knopf: New York, 1963.